Changing Perspectives
on Gender

OPEN UNIVERSITY PRESS
Gender and Education Series

Editors
ROSEMARY DEEM
*Lecturer in the School of Education at the
Open University*

GABY WEINER
*Principal Lecturer in Education at
South Bank Polytechnic*

The series provides compact and clear accounts of relevant research and practice in the field of gender and education. It is aimed at trainee and practising teachers, and parents and others with an educational interest in ending gender inequality. All age-ranges will be included, and there will be an emphasis on ethnicity as well as gender. Series authors are all established educational practitioners or researchers.

TITLES IN THE SERIES

Changing Perspectives on Gender

NEW INITIATIVES
IN SECONDARY EDUCATION

EDITED BY

Helen Burchell and Val Millman

Open University Press
Milton Keynes · Philadelphia

Open University Press
Celtic Court
22 Ballmoor
Buckingham MK18 1XW

and
1900 Frost Road, Suite 101,
Bristol, PA 19007, USA

First Published 1989. Reprinted 1990

Copyright © Editors and Contributors 1989

All rights reserved. No part of this publication may be reproduced, stored in a retrieval system or transmitted in any form or by any means, without written permission from the publisher.

British Library Cataloguing in Publication Data

Changing perspectives on gender:
   new initiatives in secondary education — (Gender in education).
   1. Great Britain. Secondary education – Sociological perspectives
   Burchell, Helen   II. Millman, Val
   III. Series
   373.41
   ISBN 0–335–09533–X

Library of Congress Cataloging-in-Publication Data

Changing perspectives on gender: new initiatives in secondary
education/edited by
   Helen Burchell and Val Millman.
   p. cm — (Gender and education series)
   Bibliography: p.
   Includes index.
   ISBN 0–335–09533–X
   1. Sex discrimination in education—Great Britain. 2. Education,
Secondary—Great Britain, 3. Educational equalization—Great Britain.
I. Burchell, Helen R. II. Millman, Val. III. Series.
LC212.83.G7G46   1988
370.19'345—dc19   88–19687   CIP

Printed in Great Britain by J. W. Arrowsmith Ltd., Bristol

Contents

Contributors

Daryl Agnew	Advisory Teacher for Equal Opportunities (Gender), Sheffield LEA
Hilary Anslow	Equal Opportunities Project Officer, Tameside LEA
Margaret Booth	Adviser for Inservice Training, Barnsley LEA; formerly Curriculum Development Officer, Sheffield LEA Curriculum Development Initiative
Helen Burchell	Principal Lecturer, School of Humanities and Education, Hatfield Polytechnic
David Dickinson	Equal Opportunities Project Officer, Rochdale LEA
Carol James	Senior Careers Officer (TVEI), Hertfordshire LEA
Patsy Kane	School Co-ordinator for Language across the Curriculum, Sheffield LEA
Jackie Kearns	Executive Director, Assessment, Inner London Education Authority; formerly Co-ordinator of Profile and London Record of Achievement Pilot Scheme
Eleanor Leitch	Assistant Headteacher, Sheffield LEA
Val Millman	Teacher Adviser, Equal Opportunities (Gender), Coventry LEA
Gaby Weiner	Staff Tutor, Open University, London Region
Jane Young	Deputy Headteacher, Hertfordshire LEA

Acknowledgements

We should like to thank Gaby Weiner and Rosemary Deem for their support and help with the preparation of this book. We would also like to acknowledge the contribution of all those whose work on gender equality has been drawn on in this book — both through their involvement in local projects and in wider developments in this field.

Helen Burchell
Val Millman

Series Editor's Introduction

In 1983, the Manpower Services Commission (MSC) signalled the first commitment at national level to equality between the sexes in education by including a criterion for funding concerning the avoidance of sex-stereotyping in its influential new programme, the Technical and Vocational Educational Initiative (TVEI). This project was also significant in that it displayed characteristics that were to be features of other government schemes being established at the time. For instance, it represented greater intervention by the government into curriculum matters, new frameworks for change, and more overtly targeted forms of funding.

This book, the sixth in the Gender and Education series, considers ways in which ideas and practices concerning equality between the sexes have developed in recent government schemes, in particular, the Lower Attaining Pupils Programme (LAPP), the aforementioned TVEI, Records of Achievement and TVEI-Related Inservice Training (TRIST). These are new developments in the field of gender since there are clear contradictions between the 'market-led' orientations of the government schemes and the egalitarian aims of former equal opportunities and anti-sexist initiatives, outlined in earlier books in the Gender and Education series.

The editors explore these contradictions by focusing on the new models of change adopted by the schemes, and then, through five case-studies, examining their commitment to, and impact on, equal opportunities generally.

It is clear that we are entering a new era in terms of work on equal opportunities. Decreasing are the more 'radical' commitments to sexual and social equality on the part of local education authorities such as, for instance, Inner London Education Authority (ILEA) and

Brent. On the other hand a number of local authorities, for instance
Sheffield and Coventry, still continue to display a firm, if somewhat
cautious, commitment to equal opportunities. And undoubtedly on
the increase is support for widening employment opportunities for
girls and women as a means of contributing to the regeneration of the
economy and wealth creation. This book is valuable in opening up
discussion of these issues, and represents a significant and welcome
contribution to the literatures of vocational education, feminist
studies and educational change.

Gaby Weiner

Introduction

> A great deal of progress has been made during the last decade and the issues surrounding sex differentiation in the curriculum and sex discrimination in education are widely understood. Understanding is essential but it does not necessarily promote change. Strategies for change are needed now and as long as change is dependent upon principle and personal commitment, a coherent national policy for equality of opportunity in education will not emerge. (Carr, 1985, p. 164)

Ten years on from the Sex Discrimination Act of 1975, Lynda Carr, Principal Education Officer of the Equal Opportunities Commission, was calling for 'strategies for change'. During this period, understanding of the issues in educational circles had indeed increased, but 'principle and personal commitment' were still the main impetus for positive action in this area. In what ways can the strategies for change that have been evolving in some schools and LEAs in the mid-1980s be sustained and developed through future secondary education initiatives, particularly at a time when the whole education system is in a period of rapid and far-reaching change?

It was this question that prompted us to consider some of the implications of these initiatives for the pursuit of greater gender equality. In this period, change has in large measure been at the instigation of central government, concerned to redirect the education offered to those in later years of secondary schools and to re-establish a greater degree of control over the system (Hopkins, 1986). The four national initiatives focused upon within this book – the Lower Attaining Pupils Programme (LAPP), Records of Achievement, Technical and Vocational Education Initiative (TVEI) and TVEI-Related Inservice Training (TRIST) – have involved large

numbers of LEAs, schools, teachers and students in the local projects they have spawned. Although there are other national developments (e.g. GCSE, CPVE) which also have significant implications for secondary school curricula, these four initiatives have a distinctive approach to bringing about change. This reflects a new relationship between central and local government expressed as a 'contract' between the two partners. Each of these initiatives is described in some detail in Chapter 1 where the author identifies the key features of the model for change underpinning them all. She also raises questions about the implications of such a model for those seeking to work for greater gender equality within these initiatives.

It is useful to view opportunities for exploring gender issues within these national initiatives against a background of developments in this area over the decade or so since the Sex Discrimination Act was passed. There is certainly now a number of LEAs which have shown concern for gender equality through policies or curriculum statements, working parties and local networks of support, development of resource banks and inservice training programmes. Some of these LEAs have appointed education officers, advisers or advisory teachers with responsibility for equal opportunities (gender). There are national organizations such as the Equal Opportunities Commission (EOC), Women's National Commission (WNC), and the School Curriculum Development Committee (SCDC) which have supported projects, published material, contributed to policy deliberations, including those surrounding the 'Great Education Reform Bill'. The increasing academic interest in gender issues and the publication of research findings has made a vital contribution to both educational debate and positive action. There have been major projects concerned principally with gender issues [e.g. Girls into Science and Technology (GIST), Girls and Technology Education (GATE) and the EOC/SCDC Equal Opportunities in Education Development Project], which have provided resources such as project teams with relevant expertise, inservice opportunities and time for teachers to engage in development work within their own schools. Although there may not be consensus about precise equal opportunities outcomes and goals, it is no longer in question whether or not gender equality is a legitimate educational issue. This position has been reached in a relatively short period of time and the various strategies developed by those involved in this process are described by Weiner in the first part of Chapter 7.

However, it would be naive to assume that these achievements signify a groundswell of sustained and active concern among teachers and educational policy-makers which is here to stay. Rather, it may suggest that those 'with principle and personal commitment' have seized what opportunities exist to make equal opportunities more visible as a legitimate area for debate and activity. But they have often had limited success in persuading others to prioritize the issues and to engage in the detailed analysis and planning necessary to begin to have a significant impact on the real opportunities available to female and male students. As has been argued by Weiner and Arnot (1987), many of the most committed teachers are not in management roles at middle or senior levels and their spheres of influence and opportunities to initiate change are therefore relatively small. Attempts to bring equal opportunity issues before the whole staff of a school are often frustrated by lack of time to give them due consideration; in the hurly-burly of normal school life the staff meeting 'discussion' or working party report can easily be passed over in favour of more pressing matters! Moreover, even in local authorities with equal opportunities policies, the degree of commitment and resourcing of equal opportunities programmes varies considerably. In a few cases, strong commitment has led to policy statements being backed by sufficient resources (advisory staff, inservice courses, school-based INSET) to ensure their implementation; in others there has been a degree of tokenism exemplified by Taylor (1987) in the appointment by an LEA of an advisory teacher for gender equality as an 'ad hoc and not too expensive response to a bit of local pressure' (p. 17).

New national initiatives seeking to promote major developments within schools offer a new stimulus for change; the opportunity for placing gender equality on schools' agendas through its incorporation in such new initiatives clearly merits exploration. One of the potential benefits of the local projects spawned by these central initiatives is a greater stimulus to schools to reflect upon their curricula and organizational patterns as they differentially affect female and male students. This stimulus is considerably strengthened by the provision of sufficient resources – time and expertise – to render this process useful and productive. Weighed against this must be the potential disadvantages of linking work on gender to initiatives which have been set up to serve central government's purposes. As Weiner argues in Chapter 7, seeking to work for greater gender equality in initiatives whose rationale is bound up with vocationalism may serve to distort significantly the direction of such work.

The central chapters within this book provide detailed accounts of how gender issues have been tackled in individual local projects as case studies of LAPP, Records of Achievement, TVEI and TRIST. They offer an opportunity to reflect upon both:

1 The particularly prominent gender issues raised in working in the area of technical and vocational education, in devising an effective curriculum for lower-attaining pupils and in developing records of achievement for all 16-year-old students; and
2 The strategies by which such issues are raised, debated and lead to plans for changes, in particular the role of inservice education for teachers in these processes.

The authors of each of the case studies in Chapters 2–5 all write as participants in one of these projects and provide us with insights into how strategies for change can evolve in a variety of contexts. In preparing these accounts, authors will obviously have been sensitive to the 'politics' of each project within the LEA and will be presenting an individual perspective.

In the Hertfordshire TVEI project (Chapter 2), whose emphasis is on new technological skills and knowledge closely matched to local employment opportunities, the authors illustrate the implications of TVEI option systems which 'compel' students to make non-traditional choices. They emphasize the importance of challenging attitudes and behaviour as well as changing structures. In this context they demonstrate the value of various forms of INSET in raising teacher awareness and instigating curricular change, although they stress that the latter is only possible if schools, and those who manage them, prioritize equal opportunities as a whole-school issue.

In Chapter 3 the description of the Sheffield LAPP project indicates how defining low attainment as a whole-school issue provided an opportunity to examine gender issues across the broadest context of the 'hidden' and 'formal' curriculum. Through their presentation of a case study of curriculum change in one of the project schools, the authors demonstrate the advantages to be gained from being able to introduce an equal opportunities perspective to an innovation from its inception. They highlight the role of senior management in prioritizing such work within the school and the significance of the allocation of teacher time for the planning, implementation and evaluation of change. Such an allocation of time was enhanced by the authority's launch of a major programme of curricular review in its schools; central to this was the secondment of teams of teachers to work on issues identified by their schools.

The area of assessment, like low attainment, is one which is still under-researched in relation to gender issues. In Chapter 4 the author offers an analysis of gender issues developed through practical experience of members of the ILEA Records of Achievement pilot project team. It is clear from her description of the project that team members were committed to gender equality from the beginning, and many of the gender issues they identified through their work have important implications for a range of assessment approaches. In particular, the author focuses upon the opportunities profiling offers for enhancing girls' self-esteem and performance. In considering strategies for change, she underlines the importance of profiling systems being part of a school assessment policy that is consonant with policies on equality of opportunity and warns against providing students with 'contradictory messages' between the 'stated and hidden curriculum'.

In contrast to the preceding three chapters, the description of Rochdale and Tameside's TRIST project in Chapter 5 concentrates exclusively on INSET as a means of promoting greater gender equality in secondary schools. The authors describe how the project used a 'power-based' model of change with a three-stage approach to training, first targeting heads, advisers and education officers, then deputy headteachers, and finally middle management/working groups of teachers. They were able to use their substantial financial backing to provide and disseminate well-resourced INSET and curriculum materials. They also discuss the potential of this intensive INSET strategy for raising awareness of gender issues and laying a strong foundation for long-term development work within LEAs.

Chapter 6 examines these four initiatives in terms of the part they have played in the development of Coventry LEA's approach to work on gender since the early 1980s. The author provides this perspective from an authority which has taken on all four initiatives, and from the basis of her longstanding involvement in the promotion of gender equality. She points to two key factors that have influenced the ways in which gender has featured in each of Coventry's projects: (1) the project parameters as defined by its funding body and (2) the LEA 'equal opportunities' climate at the time of the project's introduction. Thus the earlier projects focused on awareness-raising whereas the later ones concentrated on whole-school change strategies. In this context, particular attention is paid to the role that individuals with 'designated responsibility for gender' can play in bringing about change.

As is evident from these case studies, these four national initiatives have undoubtedly provided opportunities for work on gender equality to be initiated, reviewed and developed in contexts that differ from earlier work on gender initiated by pioneering LEAs in the early 1980s. In some projects it has been necessary for work to focus on getting the issues on to the educational agenda at project or LEA level. In others a wider awareness of the problems of inequality has been generated and the kind of action that is required has been identified. Some projects have drawn on previous work on gender to refine their strategies, e.g. in encouraging more girls into technological subjects. In projects with a high level of awareness at the outset, it has been possible to explore gender issues in previously under-researched areas, e.g. in Records of Achievement, and contribute to the growing bank of research and expertise now available.

The ways in which such opportunities have presented themselves and the extent to which they might be seen to promote gender equality successfully have been influenced in these local projects by a number of factors such as:

- the purpose and scope of the project itself;
- the climate and the context of individual LEAs;
- the existence and use of expertise on gender issues; and
- the accessibility of previous work on gender specifically relevant to the project.

Many people involved in promoting gender equality in these projects will have been faced with a sensitive, complex and at times overwhelming task. Those who are committed to bringing about significant rather than cosmetic changes in this area will have had to plan how to sustain change beyond the contractual period of the project with which they are involved. This is no easy task in the current educational climate, but as the intention was that these initiatives would, through their pilot projects, influence wider LEA practice, it is to be hoped that work on gender will become firmly lodged in school and LEA structures and policies. These projects have contributed significantly to the bank of expertise on gender issues and strategies for change in this area. We hope that this book will support those wishing to promote gender equality – teachers, headteachers, advisers, governors, LEA project teams, administrators, INSET providers – by offering further insights that will help them develop strategies within their own situations.

CHAPTER 1

Strategies for Change In New Initiatives

HELEN BURCHELL

The number of changes affecting secondary education which have been promoted by central government has increased significantly during the 1980s. In this period the responsibilities of central and local government in the management of the education service have been reformulated; as a consequence, LEAs and their schools have been involved in major reviews of their activities. The four national initiatives focused upon within this book – TVEI, LAPP, Records of Achievement and TRIST – are all examples of such centrally directed change, and they all share a particular framework within which change is to be brought about. The key feature of this framework is that the LEA becomes bound to the centrally defined objectives for the initiative through a contract with the government department or agency (DES or MSC) which is acting as sponsor; in return for 'signing the contract' significant extra funds are made available to the LEA. The precise objectives vary from initiative to initiative but they have *in common* a concern with the education of 14- to 18-year-old students, in particular how this relates to their future work roles.

For those concerned to bring about greater gender equality in schools such developments raise a number of interesting questions. What are the implications of how such initiatives seek to redefine the 14–18 curriculum for female and male students? What opportunities are there for working on gender issues within the LEA projects sponsored within each initiative? Will the typical strategies for change developed by committed teachers working in their own classrooms be in conflict with strategies for 'managing change' developed by LEA projects? Does the fact that these local pilot projects have a short time-scale within which to bring about change militate against the development of sound strategies for tackling gender issues?

In this chapter I seek to examine the scope and purposes of these initiatives at the national level, explore the framework for change which they provide and offer a critical appraisal of some of their implications for work on gender. It is my intention to examine in some detail the change process within the local projects these initiatives have spawned, so that those concerned with promoting gender equality may be in a better position to see how to capitalize upon the opportunities offered. I begin with a brief overview of the purpose and scope of the initiatives as a basis for examining the framework for change they offer.

Four initiatives: their scope and broad objectives

In setting the scene for examination of recent developments in secondary education, Hopkins (1986) points to the importance of locating these developments in their socio-political context where increasing youth unemployment and its explanation in terms of lack of appropriate skills and attitudes on the part of school leavers has led to an increase in emphasis on training. He also refers to the need to take account of an increasingly sophisticated understanding of the processes of educational change on the part of educational policy-makers. Many approaches to curriculum development and change in schools as reflected in national projects of the 1960s and 1970s had, it was argued, had only a limited effect. Schools' resistance to change needed to be overcome by alternative means. These factors have clearly influenced the ways in which DES and MSC have defined the direction for curriculum change they propose in these four initiatives; they have also affected their choice of strategy for bringing about change.

TVEI offers perhaps the clearest statement of the shift to vocationalism as its projects were set up to offer a 4-year course (14–18) of full-time general, technical and vocational education for young people across the ability range and of both sexes. The initiative has grown fast in terms of the number of LEAs involved: from 14 pilot projects in 1983 (funded by MSC at £51.5m) to the involvement of over 100 LEAs by September 1987 (with a total funding of these pilots at over £230m). Although the amount of funding for individual projects has varied (from £1.5m to £20m over 5–7 years) it has in every case been a significant addition to the funds available directly from the LEA. Typically, pilot projects involved only a proportion of an LEA's schools and within these only a proportion of the students in the cohort in question would be following a TVEI programme. Nevertheless, the number of students involved in the pilot projects was large – over 83,000 in 1987–8. The extension of TVEI beyond the pilot stage so that every school within a participating LEA will eventually be involved, and all students within these schools will have the opportunity to participate in the TVEI programme, was signalled in the White Paper. *Working Together – Education and Training* (DES/DoE, 1986), and is being funded to the tune of £900m over 10 years.

In contrast to TVEI the Lower-Attaining Pupils Programme has received only modest publicity. In the words of Penelope Weston, Project Leader of the National Evaluation Team, it is 'the Cinderella of the current 14–16 curriculum and assessment pageant' (1986). LAPP's central aim as defined by Sir Keith Joseph (Secretary of State for Education responsible for setting up the initiative) is 'to develop a better and more practical education for fourth and fifth formers who were not benefiting fully from school . . . the 40 per cent for whom public examinations were not designed' (TES, 1982). Some of the characteristics of this 'better education' include its emphasis on developing basic skills of literacy and numeracy and on the *practical* and the *relevant* (e.g. through work experience, practical projects in the community), and the fact that it would be an *alternative* curricular experience to that provided for the majority of students. Some links with the vocationalism of TVEI begin to become apparent. The LAPP programme started in the same year as TVEI, 1983, and a similar number of LEAs were involved (in this case 13) but it was funded (by DES) at a significantly lower level (£2.25m p.a.). The LAPP local projects were initially funded for 3 years with extensions of funding until 1989 in some cases; in addition, a further four LEAs joined in 1985 whose projects were scheduled to run until 1988. As in the case of the other initiatives, the number of schools, students and teachers involved has varied significantly from local project to local project.

A prime justification for DES funding of the nine Records of Achievement pilot projects is to provide a basis for the development of national guidelines for the introduction of such records for all 16-year-old students in 1995. The DES has seen the benefits of the development of such records in terms of improved student motivation, more careful identification of individual student needs, an acknowledgement of their achievements and a final record which would be valued and recognized by employers. The projects began in April 1985 and were funded initially at a total of £10 m for 3 years with extension funding already planned for a further 2 years. These nine pilot projects involved 22 LEAs, some having sole responsibility for a pilot project, others grouped together in consortia to form a single project. The number of schools involved within each LEA has varied: some have worked throughout the first phase of the project within a small number of their schools, other projects have increased the number of schools involved over this period, resulting in almost total LEA coverage. In terms of student involvement, unlike TVEI and several of the LAPP projects where discrete groups of pupils were involved in the project's work, Records of Achievement developments have been directed at involving *all* students in the relevant cohorts and, potentially, a high proportion of the teachers in each institution.

TRIST (TVEI-Related Inservice Training), the shortest-lived of the initiatives mentioned in this book, had a time-scale spanning September 1985 to April 1987 and was introduced as an 'inservice training scheme to promote developments across the curriculum of the kind related particularly to TVEI' (Barlow, 1986). It had been recognized that to achieve the aims of TVEI, further development of teachers' understanding and skills was required. There was also a further charge upon LEAs in making their bids that their submissions to MSC should be based upon a systematic assessment of inservice needs in relation to their curriculum development plans. Funded at £25 m over 5 terms, LEAs had at their disposal considerable sums of money with which to set up INSET activities, and finance supply cover for teachers engaged in them. These activities were of various kinds, ranging from 'courses' provided centrally to individual schools identifying a need and receiving finance to plan their own INSET. Likewise, the number of teachers involved in TRIST programmes and the degree of involvement varied significantly from LEA to LEA. This initiative was seen as an interim measure pending the introduction of GRIST (Grant-Related Inservice Training) in April 1987 (Barlow, 1986) and it was intended that the lessons LEAs learnt within TRIST should be a foundation for their thinking about INSET within GRIST. A key similarity between the two schemes lies in the emphasis upon 'bid' and 'contract', although GRIST later shifted the locus of control to central government through its identification of national priority areas for INSET.

As this overview has demonstrated, these initiatives clearly brought the prospect of significant changes to those LEAs which participated, but the *parameters* of the change were predefined by the broad objectives of each initiative as set nationally. A key question becomes *whose* initiatives are they? How much power does each of the partners – central government, LEA, teachers – have in shaping the local project? In the rest of this chapter I intend to explore these questions through an analysis of the key features of the model of change which, with some variations as between schemes, these initiatives may be seen to represent. I hope this analysis will enable teachers to see the points at which they might exercise greatest influence in the process of change.

A framework for change

The framework for change I propose is adapted from Harland's (1987) analysis of the mechanism of categorical funding developed by MSC for implementation of its policies in TVEI. She identified four key features: criteria against which submissions from LEAs are judged, a process of 'bidding' by LEAs, a contract between MSC and each successful LEA, and procedures for monitoring and evaluating with a view to replication. For the purposes of this chapter these features may be described as follows:

1 The LEA makes a bid for funds to the national agency charged with promotion of the initiative (MSC for TVEI and TRIST; DES for LAPP and Records of Achievement); the bid is evaluated in relation to the criteria laid down for the initiative; successful bids lead to a contract between the MSC or DES and the LEA which brings the latter significant extra funds. (This process is known as 'categorical funding'.)

2 The LEA then sets up a project team to translate its proposals into action, working with schools which have been designated or self-selected themselves to become partners in the project, and to use the extra financial resources made available to provide support for teachers through, for example, enhanced INSET opportunities.

3 The participating schools and the LEA are charged with bringing about the changes 'contracted for' and are compelled to remain accountable to the central funding agency through regular reporting procedures.

4 There is an emphasis upon evaluation of the project both through local evaluation arrangements and national evaluation teams. As the projects are essentially pilots, these evaluations are seen as the basis for the identification of issues and good practice for dissemination both locally within the LEA and nationally between LEAs.

I argue that these features can be identified within the initiatives funded by DES as well as those funded by MSC, although Harland developed the model in connection with TVEI alone and has questioned how far DES will seek to learn from MSC's success in the use of this approach.

As Harland has pointed out, there is a central paradox in this mode of policy implementation, namely strong central control coupled with an expectation of a creative response by LEAs and their schools. Thus the precise format of the project as defined by those LEAs whose bids are successful may vary. Indeed, variety is deliberately encouraged so that several different approaches can be compared – but within the parameters set by the objectives of the initiative.

Placing gender on the agenda for change

What then are the implications of these four initiatives and the model of change they provide for those concerned with achieving greater gender equality? To answer this question I will examine each feature of the model in terms of its potential contribution to the introduction or development of equal opportunities issues.

Defining the project's aims and strategy

In establishing the terms of the contract setting out the project's aims and strategy it was possible for either the funding body or the LEA to make equal opportunities a significant issue. A comparison of the TVEI initiative where equal opportunities was identified in this way by the MSC and the other initiatives where this was not so may prove illuminating. As argued earlier, since the role of the funding body is to set the *parameters* within which change is to take place, but to leave the teachers concerned to decide how this change is to be achieved, MSC did not seek to *prescribe* how the contract was to be fulfilled. This lack of clear direction undoubtedly led some teachers to question MSC's understanding of, or commitment to, equal opportunities. It also caused considerable frustration as described by

Millman and Weiner (1987). Nevertheless as Carr (1987) suggests, it can be argued that TVEI brought clear objectives and therefore methods of evaluation to equal opportunities developments. Unlike the other initiatives there was frequent, though often superficial, discussion of gender in the regular TVEI newsletter. All TVEI projects have felt a duty to be seen to address the issue in one way or another and each LEA also knew that others were obliged to do the same.

In contrast, the LAPP and Records of Achievement initiatives did not adopt an 'equal opportunities criterion' (and all that entailed in terms of monitoring, accountability and evaluation). Despite Orr's (1985) argument that there is an increasing commitment on the part of central government to gender equality, the situation presented by the role of DES in the two initiatives for which it was sponsor comes closer to the 'neutral stance' which Arnot (1987) has argued they have taken on equal opportunities issues generally.

From the local authority side, the promotion of gender issues through these projects was likely to depend upon a number of factors, not least the extent to which there was already a developed policy or clear priority given to work in this area. The short time-scales within which bids had to be prepared, and the reliance upon relatively few advisers and officers to develop them, were further factors which affected the extent to which LEAs considered the detail of project implementation and the gender implications in particular. As HMI report (DES, 1986), in the case of the LAPP projects LEAs which showed some awareness of the need to consider gender issues typically responded either in the form of general recommendations to schools to recognize and avoid sex-stereotyping or, more specifically, to select equal numbers of boys and girls to take part in project activities. Where issues such as the likely imbalance between sexes in participation in the project were not so evident, as in Records of Achievement projects, such recommendations presumably did not seem appropriate. Thus, how far LEAs considered gender issues in setting up their Record of Achievement projects is unclear, although several of the pilot LEAs either had equal opportunities policies (e.g. the ILEA) or general curriculum statements with some reference to these issues (e.g. Coventry). As Kearns indicates in Chapter 4, the existence of such a policy could create a climate which supported the project team's interests in equality issues.

The LEAs' definition of TRIST projects is equally interesting, since the *nature* of the link with TVEI was something the LEAs had to decide upon for themselves in framing their bids for MSC. It was therefore possible to assess the extent to which LEAs' experiences of gender issues in TVEI had permeated their approaches to INSET within the authority. Some LEAs (e.g. Suffolk) encouraged schools to consider equal opportunities issues in putting forward their bids for TRIST support for school-based INSET by including a reference to this in their list of criteria used to evaluate these bids. Others promoted this area by including it as a focus for LEA-led INSET (e.g. Tameside and Rochdale). However, it is disappointing to find that in the Directory of TRIST Practice (MSC, 1988) – listing some 470 activities – there is but a handful of items referring to equal opportunities.

The way in which an LEA's policy or previous work on equal opportunities affected the setting up of local projects remains an open question. While there is evidence of well-resourced policy development within which new initiatives can flourish, Headlam-Wells (1985) has pointed out how threatening to some teachers underdeveloped policies may seem, and Cant (1985) has indicated the danger of their being seen as a basis for imposition of change from above. None the less, as the Sheffield LAPP project reveals, the existence of an LEA's policy can prompt schools to give consideration to placing this issue on their agendas. In responding to these initiatives, LEAs that showed some awareness of the need to consider gender implications tended to do little more than identify the issue. Work on defining the precise nature of these implications and how to deal with them was a matter for project teams and schools.

The project team

Whatever the nature of the commitment to gender issues at the formal level reflected in the contract and the project aims, it was project teams in collaboration with the participating schools that had to shape the detail of the project. As has been argued earlier, the precise nature of the changes to be brought about would not have been prescribed by the sponsoring body. Rather, LEAs, schools and teachers had been given the parameters within which change was expected and have seen themselves as actively having to take responsibility for deciding upon the shape of the projects' activities. Project team members, individual teachers and schools that wished to take up gender issues were, therefore, provided with an opportunity to do so and the central chapters within this book reveal the ways in which such opportunities were created and developed. Change in this area is particularly sensitive and problematic and for this reason, as each of these projects bears witness, it was clearly important that project

teams included staff who had a commitment to and an understanding of gender issues. As Millman and Weiner (1987) point out
with regard to TVEI, it might be expected that project teams staffed
mainly by men with little experience of equal opportunities work
were unlikely to make gender issues central. The importance of a
clearly defined responsibility within the team for promoting
consideration of gender issues is illustrated in the case study of
Coventry's TVEI project (see Chapter 6).

The project in the school

Whether it was the project team or the schools that promoted
consideration of gender equality within the project, there remained
the question of what made some schools responsive and others not.
As Whyte (1985) has demonstrated in analysing the impact of GIST
upon schools, one critical factor is the 'climate for change' within the
participating schools. She identified as key factors a 'progressive
ethos', committed staff at senior level and a relatively high proportion of women staff at senior levels. (In Chapter 3, the Sheffield
LAPP project clearly illustrates the impact of each of these factors in
its case study of East Bank school.) How best to effect change in the
direction of greater gender equality at school level is problematic in
any event and there are continuing debates over the relative merits of
various versions of the 'top-down' or 'bottom-up' strategies for
change. The relevance of various management strategies (posts of
special responsibility, school policy statements, working parties) in
bringing about large-scale, whole-school, cross-curricular change to
effect greater gender equality needs to be carefully explored. Where
gender issues have been addressed to any depth within these projects
and the LEA concerned has used project resources to give considerable support to the proposed developments, schools have had to
consider whether to use any of these strategies for promoting greater
gender equality within the school. At the school level, what these
national initiatives have done is highlight the need to develop greater
understanding of how change is best brought about. As at LEA level,
so at school level a critical question will remain – do the aims of the
project constrain the ways in which gender inequality is tackled?

The role of INSET

What is clear, however, is that the level of staff awareness and
understanding of gender issues is a critical factor in the success of any

of these strategies for change. Each of these initiatives has provided increased opportunities for school-focused INSET. The importance of carefully targeted INSET on equal opportunities has been claimed both by Orr (1985) and by Taylor (1985):

> It is quite clear that if all pupils are to benefit from the anti-sexist insights and practice of a few teachers, then ways have to be found of extending it to many more. Equally, it is clear that simply requiring teachers to change their approach, or requiring them to discuss important policy issues when they are unprepared, or expecting them somehow suddenly to know how to behave differently in the classroom when it has taken those involved in the work many years of discussion, self-examination and trial and error to develop new approaches, is foolish and unrealistic. It is more than that: it is fatal. For the best way of ensuring that anti-sexist initiatives fail is to foist them on teachers (and others involved in education) without preparation or time to reach an understanding of the issues, and then be helpless in the face of things going wrong. The responsibility of in-service training therefore is to provide teachers with sufficient understanding and knowledge to make professional sense of the demands for change being made on them, and sufficient support to enable them to step beyond understanding into action in their schools. This is not easy, for schools as organizations are constructed to resist change. (Taylor, 1985, pp. 105–6)

Traditionally, we have been used to seeing INSET as supporting the professional development of the teacher and acknowledging it is the teacher's prerogative to decide how to translate the ideas into changed curricula. But, as Harland (1986) has observed, we may be witnessing a reversal of this process in terms of the government's perception of the role of INSET. The nature of the curriculum change is a given and the role of INSET is to help teachers to 'deliver' it. Such a stark reversal is not necessarily immediately evident in these projects but any shift in this direction clearly raises questions about ways in which INSET in the area of equal opportunities will be targeted and how its effectiveness will be assessed. For example, if teachers feel 'coerced' into INSET, will they react any differently from their students if 'coerced' into non-traditional subjects in TVEI? Will there be a focus upon changing *behaviour* rather than changing *attitudes* (cf. the TREO model examined in Chapter 5)? Furthermore, will there be a tendency to 'target' for INSET those who are seen to have *power* to bring about change rather than those *committed* to the need for change?

The importance of monitoring and evaluation

A further important feature of the framework for change which these initiatives provided was the emphasis upon monitoring and evaluation. The monitoring function served to emphasize regularly the accountability of the LEAs and their schools to the sponsoring body. Harland (1987) demonstrated how MSC had developed quite sophisticated monitoring arrangements using a network of Regional Advisers to carry its message to each LEA and to disseminate 'good practice'. By this means and others MSC has sought to present a high profile for all aspects of TVEI. As Millman and Weiner (1987) point out, the accountability of LEAs through the monitoring process undoubtedly *did* prompt LEAs and schools to attempt to bring about change. By comparison, DES monitoring and evaluation procedures may not have achieved such a high profile for their two initiatives (see Harland, 1987, for a discussion of whether it will emulate MSC in this respect).

The emphasis given to both national and local evaluation within these initiatives is also significant because it can demonstrate to the sponsoring body or to the LEA the need to address gender issues where these have been signalled within the projects. An example of this is the interim national evaluation of the pilot record of achievement projects (PRAISE, 1987), which points to the need to consider issues of gender, race and class in developing such records and thereby signals to those who *wish to listen* (hopefully, the DES!) the need to further explore this area. Within the LAPP initiative, there is some indication that local evaluations have been significant in identifying gender issues for the projects to deal with (Langley, 1986; Haywood and Wootten, 1987). However, whether or not evaluation can play this critical role is dependent upon two factors: the extent to which evaluators themselves are attuned to the need to explore gender issues and the extent to which the evaluation data, where it does reveal such issues, is taken on board seriously by those to whom the evaluations are addressed.

Moreover, evaluating equal opportunities work is not without its problems. Sound evaluation needs to be based upon clear objectives and in the case of equal opportunities projects may not have been clear in this respect. In the absence of clear objectives, there may be a tendency to evaluate solely on the basis of quantitative data, e.g. focusing narrowly upon student participation rates.

Conclusions

Change has become a central issue for the education system in the 1980s. But what makes the changes schools experience in this period different from those that went before? I have argued that for some of these a new model of change is being developed, one which represents a new form of partnership between central government, LEAs and their schools. Through this partnership central government is seeking to implement its policies with, it has been argued, an emphasis on vocationalism and accountability. LEAs for their part seek to gain significant extra funding to develop aspects of their education service. Indeed, if the areas for development represented in these initiatives *remain* ones in which central government wishes to see change brought about, then this partnership is likely to continue into the immediately foreseeable future. As Harland (1987) has argued, this model of policy implementation can serve both partners well if there is broad agreement on the principles of the proposed changes and providing teachers' commitment is achieved through giving them a powerful degree of control within the change process. Is there such broad agreement on the implications of such changes for promoting greater gender equality? If gender issues become bound up with vocationalism how will they then be defined? These questions are explored in more detail by Weiner in Chapter 7; suffice it to say here that such a link may seriously affect the task of bringing about greater gender equality if it narrows the focus to merely 'getting more girls into technology'.

Those wishing to bring about greater gender equality, at whatever level within the education service, have to decide what gains can be made through the existence of such initiatives and set their goals accordingly. Reflecting on how the model has developed to date suggests a number of possible strategies. The experience of TVEI compared with the LAPP and Records of Achievement initiatives suggests that there is clearly some argument for an 'equal opportunities criterion' built in by the funding body. Equally significant is the way in which the project is conceived and organized within the LEA. Gender issues need to be considered at every stage; when the bid is first developed, in the setting up of the project team, in the arrangements for day-to-day monitoring and steering of the project and in the criteria for the final evaluations. This signals the need to involve those with relevant knowledge and experience at each stage *as a matter of policy*. Within schools those committed to gender equality need to know how to capitalize upon the existence of these projects, to understand how such projects operate *within their institution* so that the benefits the projects bring – resources, INSET opportunities, time for school-based development – can be used to work for greater gender equality. Moreover, however small the achievements for gender equality within such projects, however limited teachers feel their understanding of the issues, it is crucially important that such achievements and understandings are made visible through the monitoring and evaluation processes. These processes form a link between teachers involved in grassroots developments and those charged with developing policy.

Acknowledgement

I would like to thank Val Millman for her useful comments and suggestions on several drafts of this chapter.

CHAPTER 2

Case Study: Equal Opportunities through the Hertfordshire TVEI Project*

CAROL JAMES AND JANE YOUNG

Technical and Vocational Education Initiative

TVEI was set up to support the development of 4-year courses (14–18) of full-time general, technical and vocational education for young people across the ability range. TVEI's first criterion was that equal opportunities should be available to young people of both sexes. The initiative was funded and managed centrally by the Manpower Services Commission (MSC).

From 14 pilot projects in 1983 the initiative had increased its scope to include over 100 LEAs by September 1987. Pilot projects typically involved only a proportion of an LEA's schools and within these only a proportion of students would follow a TVEI programme. Arrangements for TVEI extension, set up in 1987, indicate that eventually all schools within a participating LEA and all students within them will have the opportunity to participate in TVEI. The funding of the initial pilot projects was at a high level, affording significant extra financial support to LEAs and participating schools. Although the total sum set aside for TVEI extension (£900m over 10 years) is very large, it will provide a considerably lower level of support per student.

---

* The views expressed in this chapter are those of the authors and do not necessarily reflect those of the LEA.

Hertfordshire was in Phase 1 of the Technical and Vocational Education tion Initiative, and developed a highly technological project. As with all the TVEI Projects, Hertfordshire was bound by the following clause of the MSC's national criteria:

> equal opportunities should be available to young people of both sexes and they should normally be educated together on courses within each project. Care should be taken to avoid sex-stereotyping. (MSC, 1984a)

This chapter is our account of the Hertfordshire Project's response to this clause; it is our interpretation of the progress of plans and activities to meet these contractual requirements. We write as a careers officer and a deputy headteacher who have together led the activities of the Equal Opportunities Working Group, set up at the beginning of the project's third year, and our observations are based wholly on our experience of working on equal opportunities as part of the Hertfordshire TVEI Project. The interpretation of events offered in this chapter is a personal one and does not seek to represent the views of the LEA or project team.

The account we present probably echoes many of the concerns, frustrations, achievements that others have met in working on gender issues in TVEI, working in a context where the contractual requirements showed little awareness of the extent of the issues. What we seek to present in this chapter is an account of how a significant number of subject teachers, guidance teachers and careers officers involved in TVEI, including ourselves, came to realize the complexity of the task. We aim to demonstrate this growth in understanding and the various strategies developed, by describing first of all the nature of the Hertfordshire TVEI Project and its context, followed by an account of the changing emphases of activities to tackle the problem through the years.

For the first 2 years of the project, certain strategies were implemented to ensure equal provision and, as far as possible, equal take-up in schools of the TVEI options. It is at the end of this period that we, and a small group of teachers from the TVEI schools, became more involved in the issues, and the second half of this chapter details our activities.

The Hertfordshire Project in context

When the Hertfordshire submission for participation in the Technical and Vocational Education Initiative was written in 1983, it was centred on the town of Stevenage, with all 10 secondary schools participating. The 'high-tech' aims of the submission matched well a sector of the local employment scene, and the close geographical proximity of schools to each other aided in some measure a corporate identity, which the TVEI Project aimed to establish. From the beginning it had a highly technological slant; indeed one of its aims was for pupils to have access to expanding areas of new technological skills and knowledge and to apply these through practically orientated courses.

The new town of Stevenage has a population of 75,000, and recently celebrated its fortieth anniversary from its beginnings as the first New Town in 1946. The industrial and commercial activity in the town's industrial areas includes electronic, electrical and mechanical engineering, some manufacturing, life assurance, administrative offices for national and international firms, and a comprehensive provision of service industries, such as retail, catering, leisure, and a large District General Hospital.

The research and development work being carried out by some of the major local companies into electronics, communications, software, and weapons technology ensures that within Stevenage there is a range of forward-looking initiatives into which private companies are investing money and expertise. Recruitment and training are major concerns in these large firms and they present an active and interested front to the many forms of school–industry liaison. Stevenage Borough Council has always demonstrated a high level of commitment to attracting and retaining companies. Also, in conjunction with the MSC, the Council supported the setting up of the Stevenage ITeC, an information technology centre whose primary functions include a Youth Training Scheme for training in office-based computer technology and electronics.

The neighbouring towns of Letchworth, Welwyn Garden City and Hatfield have a similar concentration of 'high-tech' industries, and the workforce is usually mobile, with many skilled and semi-skilled workers moving between the towns. These towns are within the London commuter belt, and easy access to London via the Al(M) or by rail enables a sizeable minority of the working population to travel to London each day.

The population of the town has a higher than average proportion of young people (over 20 per cent of the population of Stevenage is aged under 20 years old). This school population was served by six

co-educational, two girls' and two boys' secondary schools in 1983.
These are all 11–18 comprehensive schools and in 1983 had a total
fifth year population of 1416. At the start of the project they offered
broadly similar curricula programmes and were grouped geographi-
cally in consortia for sixth form courses, ensuring that students
could choose from a wider range of courses than those available at
only one school. Employment prospects for young people in the
town are not varied, but there is ample choice for a young person
with some qualifications to enter directly into employment, mainly
engineering or office/commercial work. Many are offered jobs in
retail, catering and leisure outlets, and some enter the construction
industry. On the whole, local organizations present a typical picture of traditional female and male work roles, though there are
a few exceptions. Almost all of these employment opportunities
for young people include training, and there is a much wider range
of activities available for young people via the Youth Training
Scheme. At the end of their participation in the Scheme in 1987,
over 70 per cent of trainees were offered, or found, permanent
employment.

This description of the local economy serves to explain in part the
nature of the Hertfordshire Project. Its emphasis on new technological skills/knowledge is reflected in the titles of the TVEI options
offered – Computer Studies, Manufacturing Technology, Modular
Technology, Electronic Instrumentation, Information Technology,
and Office Technology and Communications. These last two were
taught with Industrial Studies. All courses were taught using new
modern equipment, much of it computer-linked, in refurbished
classrooms and technology workshops. For all of the first year of the
project and, for some schools, part of the second year, while building adaptations were under way, many pupils were taught in
specially-equipped buses. All the courses were taught in the first year
by a central team of specialist teachers, visiting each school. Several
of these teachers were, at the same time, developing a syllabus for
the new courses and preparing examinations. A careers officer was
seconded full-time from the County Careers Service, with responsibility for setting up a work experience programme with local
employers, and for leading developments in guidance work in the
schools.

Each school was to offer the new package of courses to 32 pupils to
facilitate splitting for option groups. This requirement, that the
resources should be devoted to a designated cohort of pupils in each

school, was laid down by MSC as part of its monitoring process, since an object of the pilot schemes was to ascertain the cost of curriculum change per pupil if an extension of the scheme were later to be desired.

These pupils chose three of their options from the following combination:

- Computer Studies or Manufacturing Technology;
- Electronic Instrumentation or Modular Technology;
- Office Technology and Communications or Information Technology.

A pupil had to opt in for the whole package; no pupils were allowed to follow just one or two of the courses. As well as these three options, the pupils in the cohort took two or three other options from their school programme, and all the compulsory subjects such as Maths, English, Careers, PE, etc. All pupils in the TVEI cohort had 2 weeks of work experience, planned and arranged specifically to relate to one or more of the TVEI subjects they were studying and, at the end of the fifth year, each pupil received a summative profile for each TVEI subject studied and a record of their work experience.

Equal opportunities in the first 2 years

The Hertfordshire TVEI Project was bound to the national criteria for all TVEI projects, including the provision of equal opportunities. The LEA itself in 1983 had no clearly stated position on equal opportunities, though since that time the County Council has drawn up an Equal Opportunities Policy which is now in effect. One important aspect of equal opportunities is equality of 'resources', and in Stevenage the provision of equal resources under TVEI was facilitated by an expensive programme of building adaptations and the installation of equipment. Each school was then able to offer the courses under its own roof, whether co-educational or single sex, and in the latter case this was particularly significant for the development of technology at one of the all girls' schools. The team of specialist teachers visited each school to teach the new subjects, and began at the same time an extensive programme of INSET to introduce the new subjects to school-based staff, many of whom were able to take on the teaching of TVEI subjects to the 1984 fourth-year cohort in their own schools. Centrally-based TVEI teaching staff continued to teach their subjects in schools where there were no staff trained in the subjects, but very early on the project began to see success in this exercise which enabled schools to offer all courses, another important move in ensuring equality of resource in the schools.

The task of attracting girls and boys in equal numbers to take up the TVEI options proved difficult. The project expected the co-educational schools to try to ensure that their cohorts included an equal representation of girls and boys, and single-sex schools were expected to ensure that all TVEI options were offered, and all taken up.

During the first 2 years the effect of the restrictions imposed by the cohort pattern of funding became apparent. The funding enabled each school to offer the three sets of TVEI options to a discrete group of 32. Co-educational schools were expected to aim at a cohort of 16 girls and 16 boys, with each option group including 8 girls and 8 boys. No school achieved this for both the 1983 and 1984 cohorts, and very few achieved it at all. In some cases the cohorts were very unbalanced, and in all these cases they included more boys than girls

Table 1 TVEI options: 1983 and 1984 entry

Subject	1983		1984	
	Girls	Boys	Girls	Boys
Manufacturing Technology	53	99	55	86
Computer Studies	67	84	65	95
Modular Technology	55	91	58	90
Electronic Instrumentation	65	92	58	95
Information Technology	38	110	48	105
Office Technology and Communications	82	73	77	72

(see Table 1). However, given the situation prior to the introduction of the TVEI subjects in schools, when there were *no* girls studying technological options, and *no* boys studying office skills courses, these first two cohorts included some pupils in each school who for the first time were embarking on non-traditional courses.

It was clear that the point of entry to the project, that is the third year options choice programme, needed attention in order to make the pupils aware of the content, style and opportunities available in the new courses, especially as a non-traditional subject. In some schools, all third year pupils were interviewed, sometimes with their parents, by a senior member of staff. In other schools, only those pupils who had expressed an interest in studying one or more of the TVEI options were interviewed. At this stage, an introduction to the new subjects was limited to an entry in a school options booklet, and perhaps a talk by a teacher of the subject. In all schools all pupils had the opportunity to talk over their options choice and career plans with a Careers Officer.

The TVEI subjects were successful in the schools to the extent that there was little difficulty in recruiting pupils. It was clear that boys were in the majority in opting for most of the subjects, perhaps because they identified with them more readily than the girls, in terms of experience, familiarity, expectations and family pressure. However, the proportion of girls opting for the subjects in the first 2 years was a big step from the situation of total non-participation in non-traditional subjects pre-TVEI. It was still a matter for concern that five out of the six TVEI subjects were more readily accepted by the boys than the girls, especially considering that the structuring of the TVEI options meant that, in order to study one TVEI option, a pupil had to choose two other TVEI options. Therefore, for example, a girl choosing to explore one non-traditional subject may also have accepted a subject she did not want to study.

Much has been written about the value of compulsion in ensuring that girls and boys receive equal educational opportunities (Luxton, 1986). The case for compulsion recognizes that boys and girls do not approach option choice from the same point of experience and background, and that the problem of making an unbiased choice at the age of 13 is compounded by family and social pressures to conform to a stereotyped image of one's own sex. The reduction or removal of choice ensures that girls and boys then follow a very similar range of courses, and do not disadvantage themselves by opting out of scientific or technological subjects which might be needed for career opportunities later on. Compulsion can only work effectively if, at the same time, staff are consciously assessing their own classroom practices and language for sexist messages, and pupils themselves are experiencing awareness-raising exercises, perhaps via a social education programme, to help them deal with the messages they are receiving at home.

It is undoubted that during the third year options choice programme some girls received some pressure, in the form of directive guidance, from senior staff who had very clearly in mind their end result of an equal numerical balance of girls and boys. In interviews with some of these girls, and some boys, it has become clear that motivation and interest was low in the third option, which they chose often just to ensure they were able to study their two other TVEI options. This is not peculiar to the Hertfordshire TVEI Project, and may be seen in any school where pupils are given the opportunity to choose subjects, but at the same time the school has to reconcile staffing, classroom space, equipment available and viable option group size.

The destinations of these pupils post-16 did not show a marked difference due to the influence of a more concentrated technical education than their non-TVEI peers. Although based only on the fifth year destinations of pupils leaving school in 1985, a comparison of the first TVEI cohort and the rest of the town's fifth year pupils shows that, of the TVEI pupils entering work, training or further education in a commercial/secretarial activity, 33 per cent were male, and of non-TVEI pupils, 21 per cent were male. A similar analysis of pupils entering engineering work, training or further education shows that 3 per cent of TVEI pupils entering engineering were female, compared with 12 per cent of non-TVEI pupils. These figures should be treated with some care as the numbers of pupils involved are small.

On the other hand, when restrictions were lifted in 1985, allowing any number of pupils to choose up to two TVEI options, and three new subjects were introduced (Vocational French, Food Industries, and Graphic and Product Design), numerical evidence of sex-stereotyping became more apparent than ever. Many schools were now running two or three option groups of Office Technology and Communications, with a large majority of girls. Of the three new courses, girls identified with Vocational French and Food Industries, and the Graphic and Product Design option attracted largely an equal number of girls and boys. Still, the five options which had been dominated by the boys in 1983 and 1984 did not attract the girls and, with the removal of the restrictions, the numbers of girls participating in non-traditional subjects dropped further. The highest participation was from the two all-girls' schools. One of those schools in particular had appointed a female Head of Technology to teach the Manufacturing Technology and Modular Technology options, and with a specific responsibility to develop a junior technology course for all pupils in years 1–3.

Throughout these early years, activities to tackle stereotyped attitudes were concentrated on the pupils themselves. They were encouraged to understand that they could study these new courses in their own school, taught by teachers whom they knew, and were given individual guidance to help them define their own interests, aspirations, strengths and weaknesses, in relation to all the option subjects. In addition, many schools were beginning to look at lower-school technology, and information technology courses, and some were beginning to offer taster courses for third year pupils. However, these moves alone could not counter the influence of their parents, peers, society and teacher attitudes in maintaining the traditional roles and expectations of girls and boys they had experienced so far in their lives. School and project staff were aware of these influences, and it is certain that some work with parents and with teachers would have been planned, if there had been no resistance from teaching staff on industrial action. (It was very difficult to hold parents' consultation evenings, which for 2 or 3 years were often attended poorly or not at all by teachers. A compromise was to hold them in the afternoon, though this meant that fewer parents were able to attend.)

However, it is doubtful whether at this stage in the project there was full awareness of the implications of equal opportunities. One reason for this was that the in-service training programme offered by the TVEI Project staff to school-based staff was badly affected by industrial action. Much of this training was planned to take place after school hours, but limited participation by staff suggested that, where possible, staff should have access to in-service training during school hours. Towards the end of the second year of the project, a concerted programme was drawn up for the exam and post-exam period of June and July, when staff and rooms became available in schools. This training was an essential introduction to the new equipment, course aims and objectives and new teaching and learning styles, and a great deal of work needed to be carried out with staff completely new to the experience of TVEI. While many of the TVEI Project staff were themselves aware of gender bias in their own subjects, and were personally able to identify this, the pressures on them and staff in schools meant that equal opportunities was not given a high priority, nor was an integrated approach taken to it. There was no forum to which information and concerns could be brought for discussion.

This then was the position regarding equal opportunities in the project at the end of the first 2 years; a few teachers, both school- and project-based, with a greater understanding of and commitment to the issues, but in general a relatively low awareness on the part of the teachers of the complexity of the issues, and at the time few opportunities for in-service training to bring the problem to the attention of more staff.

We now begin to show how our involvement with other representatives from the schools began a period of new activities, focusing the issues on the different groups of people involved, and the way in which they could each begin to get to grips with the problem in their own way.

A shift in focus

An opportunity to reassess our own position and attitudes towards equal opportunities came in the summer of 1985, with a series of workshops organized by TVEI Hertfordshire, Enfield and Bedfordshire, and run by external management consultants. The aims of the workshops were (a) to raise awareness in the area of equal opportunities, and (b) to develop a 'delivery model'. It gave the opportunity for small teams of teachers from each school to attend, supporting each other.

The workshops opened with identifying barriers which we believed existed to prevent us offering and achieving equal opportunities in schools, and consideration of different methods which would make us more effective in the provision of equal opportunities. As barriers, the participants identified some outside school – parental attitudes, employers' attitudes, young people themselves, accepted social practice – and some within schools – organizational structure, staff attitudes, lack of resources, staff promotion policies.

As ways of moving forward, we were offered the following models, as developed by The Prospect Centre (MSC, 1984b, 1985):

1 The unlocked door – 'We're not blocking your path'.
2 The open door – 'Welcome aboard'.
3 The special escalator – 'All aboard'.
4 Equal outcomes – 'We'll see you there'.

The second stage of the workshop highlighted personal skills (such as assertiveness training and negotiating skills) to enable the participants to be more successful in achieving a satisfactory outcome. It also gave the opportunity for more intensive work on some of the key areas of concern such as option choices, profiling and social education programmes.

With the final stage of the workshop came the need to make decisions about our future activity in the area of equal opportunities, i.e. where we would concentrate our efforts. Since the course had enabled us to see the issues now in the much broader terms of attitudes, information and action, it seemed clear that any future activities to improve the provision of equal opportunities within TVEI would need to include activity for the whole school, and would require us to look at equal opportunities from a more fundamental starting point, a different approach from that which had been held at the start of the project, when perhaps the difficulties of making significant progress had not been fully realized.

Working group

The most immediate outcome of this opportunity for reflection was the setting up of a working group to support existing work going on within schools, formed to represent the schools in the north of the town – the schools who had been fully represented at the workshop and who, it was felt, could form a pilot group for the rest of the town. This initial group, of which we were both members, included two representatives from each school, who would meet regularly and plan and evaluate activities. These, it was thought, might include such things as surveys of option sixth form choices, research on materials and social education programmes.

There was a tremendous sense of enthusiasm among those involved at this stage for taking the work on equal opportunities forward, plus the invaluable support from TVEI to enable teachers to meet within the school's day, during a period when most inservice activities were being squeezed out. The schools represented were an interesting mixture, and unusual for the town, being one co-educational comprehensive, one boys' comprehensive, and boys' and girls' Roman Catholic comprehensives. The group's members ranged from scale 1 to deputy headteachers – some chosen by headteachers, and some self-appointed because of commitment in this area.

Group meetings began in the Autumn of 1985, and it was strongly felt that we needed as much data as possible which had relevance for equal opportunities in the schools, if we were to be able to go to colleagues and convince them that here was an issue which needed serious consideration. The minutes of the first meeting set out the areas for research:

(a) Fourth and Fifth Year option choices
   (i) Survey of option choices (preferably going back five years, and showing the percentage of boys or girls taking each subject).
   (ii) Investigation of the arrangement of option groups, the rationale behind them, and the consequences of them.

(b) Sixth Form choices
   (i) 'A' level choices of boys/girls.
   (ii) An account of any vocational courses on offer, highlighting any implications for a curriculum based on Equal Opportunities.

(c) Destinations of school leavers – looking at first destinations of pupils at 16 and 18, over a three year period.

(d) Staffing
   (i) A statistical investigation of the ratio of women to men on staff lists, and the distribution of scales and posts of responsibility.
   (ii) A closer investigation into the particular roles men/women perform in schools.

It was also considered vital that the headteachers were involved as much as possible, perhaps to set up a working party within each school, to make available to all staff the collected data, and certainly to put equal opportunities on the 'accepted agenda' of each school.

Once collected, the data made depressing reading. There was no sign that pupils felt less restricted by sex-stereotyped choices of subjects and careers than they had before TVEI; in almost all cases, pupils were conforming to stereotyped roles, and it seemed to us highly unlikely that they had been able to make a free and informed choice, without facing restraints of various kinds. This could be seen in the traditionally 'male' and 'female' options remaining just that, with single-sex schools conforming to this same pattern, and in the careers pupils were entering. Additionally, it was clear that they were being educated in a system where the adult role models about them contrived to reinforce in the most public way the idea that women's work is less highly valued than men's, as could be seen clearly in the roles and responsibilities of female and male staff.

The group felt that they had the necessary evidence now to show that we were failing to achieve equal opportunities for our staff and our pupils, and that the best ways of moving forward were:

1 To communicate the data to as many people as possible in order to extend awareness of this issue; and
2 To work towards the collection of resources, physical and human, which we could use and make available to others in our work on equal opportunities.

The data was sent to all schools and headteachers, to local colleges and employers as well as LEA officials. In its own way this period highlighted the difficulty of tackling the issue of equal opportunities; there were no official responses to the data at all, and within staff-rooms, where verbal responses did come, they ranged from the anti-pathy felt by some for anything bearing an equal opportunities tag, through the 'but that's life' response, to the indignation of those perceiving this as an important problem area for schools. At least within staffrooms though, equal opportunities was appearing as an item on each of the schools' agendas – however welcome or unwelcome.

The working group went on to collect and make available resources: display materials suitable for promoting equal oppor-tunities were investigated and the information circulated, as was a list of organizations offering women and men speakers in non-traditional roles. School libraries were asked to mount displays of books related to equal opportunities, and teaching staff were asked to help complete a textbook survey.

All these activities continued to raise the profile of equal oppor-tunities in the schools, but there was a strong feeling that our real need was to get more staff within each school involved in the activi-ties, to take on board equal opportunities as an issue for which they had some responsibility. The problems of getting people together during a period of industrial action continued to be frustrating. Informal coffee-time meetings where information and ideas could be exchanged, were tried in one school with some success, but it still felt like 'scratching the surface'.

Day Workshop, June 1986

However, a commitment had been given to the TVEI Project when the North Stevenage group met initially to hold a day workshop for representatives from all the secondary schools in Stevenage, and this gave a new opportunity to extend our work to a wider group of people. Represented at the workshop were teams from all the TVEI schools, Stevenage College, the Careers Service, and TVEI staff. The day aimed to raise awareness of some of the issues of equal opportunities by:

1 Asking each group to make an initial statement about the situation regarding equal opportunities in their institutions.
2 Considering the blockages which exist to achieving equal opportunities.
3 Looking at ways of overcoming those blockages.
4 Looking at some of the areas identified in more detail, coming up with some practical ideas for improvement.
5 Arranging within each of the town's consortia to pick up the issues of the day for future discussion and activities.

The successes of the day were the new scale of involvement of other professionals concerned with young people, and the commitment to pick up the issues raised for future work. This commitment, which came from all the secondary schools in the town, led to two new working groups being formed on the same pattern as the North Stevenage group, based on existing consortia.

The consortium-based working groups began to meet and two major concerns emerged: option choices, which newly collected data suggested were as stereotyped as ever, and staffing policies, particularly highlighted by the imminent amalgamation of the four single-sex schools in the town into two co-educational schools. On option choices, while there was a certain level of despondency about the influences other than school which affected pupils' choices, it was agreed that merely providing an apparent 'free choice' or 'open door' was not enough, and that more needed to be done. As a starting point, members of the working parties collected schemes and ideas from other schools, LEAs and TVEI projects. The Careers Service agreed to take a fresh look at careers conventions, with regard to displays and representatives, and to make equal opportunities material available to parents; TVEI staff mounted a mobile exhibition promoting non-stereotyped option choices, which schools could borrow for parents' evenings; the schools put on 'taster' lessons for pupils in unfamiliar subjects, organizing the pupils into single-sex groups to attend these; and it was agreed that more individual and group counselling of pupils should take place.

On the staffing issues, the amalgamations had raised many fears among staff: if the pattern of male seniority in schools was to be strengthened with the demise of the two girls' schools, then how could we as teachers expect our pupils to take the issue of equal opportunities seriously when we were ourselves so obviously part of an unequal system? The anxieties of all the staff in the amalgamating schools were very real, but figures such as those collected in North Stevenage which highlighted the significantly weaker starting point for many of the women involved, made them in particular fear for their prospects in the new schools. There emerged a need for some of those involved to have time to consider their own positions, both in their career and their life generally, to have time to draw support from each other, and to acquire some skills which might see them through new staff selection procedures. This led to a request for a weekend conference for women teachers.

Personal Effectiveness Course for Women, March 1987

The working groups contributed their ideas for the planning of the weekend course, and once the TVEI Project's full support, including financial, had been given, we (the authors) set about the organization. Joining us in the planning and delivery of the weekend was an adviser with experience of running courses for women teachers who was known to many of our colleagues because of her contribution at the day workshop. We decided to share the leadership of the weekend between us, not because we were experts but because we felt it was essential to build up a supportive atmosphere for us all, without some of the anxieties that visiting speakers can bring.

We felt it to be very important that the weekend concentrated on personal effectiveness, and this became the title of the course – to allow each participant the opportunity to reflect on many aspects of her life, including, but not only, work. Setting the course in a hotel was also seen as critical – the participants needed to feel that their time and efforts were being valued. The course was made open to women teachers in all the secondary schools, the Stevenage TVEI central staff, and Careers Officers, and over 30 women attended.

All the participants felt that their own personal worth and value was being recognized, by the surroundings and facilities the course offered – an excellent example of 'the dignity of INSET experiences'. The first day's programme gave the women the opportunity to reflect on their own strengths, and set themselves goals. This was supported by assertiveness training on the second day. The positive response from the participants highlighted just how rarely women get the opportunity to consider their own careers, and how much they value support and skills training. Many people left the weekend feeling much more confident at being able to promote equal opportunities for themselves and their pupils. The impact of our work on personal effectiveness had led to more professional confidence. One follow-up of the work was the decision by one of the girls' schools to put more effort and time on a school-wide basis into assertiveness training. Subsequently, a series of workshops for the staff on assertiveness was held.

Where are we now?

At this stage in the work, the consortium groups across the town decided to merge into one working group. The usefulness and activities of this new group have been the subject, among its own members, of much discussion. The group itself obviously cannot change internal school policies, nor more individual attitudes. Much of the most important work has to be done at school level. Examples were already being highlighted. The new, greatly reduced option scheme in one of the newly amalgamated schools was felt to be a major step forward in beginning to eliminate stereotyped option choices; one headteacher who was critically examining his staffing policies and appointments was engendering great confidence among the female teaching staff in their career prospects. But it was felt that the group could valuably continue its activities on general issues, or subject-specific issues, by continuing to collect data on matters such as pupil choices/destinations, by acting as a pressure group on the staffing issue and, overall, by continuing to give equal opportunities a high profile.

INSET activities remain an important strategy. A second one-day workshop for teams of teachers, Careers Officers and TVEI staff took place in June 1987. The aim for this workshop was to give individual participants the confidence to feel that they had a positive and powerful role to play in improving equal opportunities for their students, even if their institution was not moving along as fast as they would wish. Personal practice with regards to classroom inter-action, discipline and report writing and marking was examined. A critical reassessment of our own attitudes was undertaken, and models of setting personal goals, and school goals, were offered. The day again sparked off great enthusiasm, and seemed to hit the right note in encouraging individuals to be positive and set themselves targets.

Other INSET activities have included work with Business Educa-tion teachers and CDT teachers, with several other subject-based workshops planned. On the staffing issue, the co-ordinating group has collected more data on career progression to support its work, and discussions about the situation have started to take place with those people able to affect change in this area, although this is an area of some tension.

A continuing aim is to bring headteachers more closely into the work, by reporting regularly to them, asking for their support and ideas. Each member of the co-ordinating group aims to report and discuss issues with them regularly, and all information on data and courses is directed to them. The need for their committed support cannot be overestimated.

Perhaps one of the most important lessons we have learned over the later stages of our activity, is that we now need seriously to take the issues back to the pupils. They need to perceive the need for a change in school policies and their own educational choices. If they perceive no need, just as if the teachers perceive no need, what chance is there of any breakthrough? There is a commitment to increase pupils' involvement in the issue through social education programmes, assemblies, preparation for option choices, and work experience and profiling. We must share our concern over collected data with the pupils: we must make equal opportunities a 'live' issue for them as it is for us.

Conclusion

At the time of writing we are 4 years into the project, and equal opportunities still seems, in many ways, to be as far off as ever. In our most despairing moments it has the manner of an issue which gets harder to tackle the more you understand it. Yet in a way, the many teachers and other professionals who have been involved with the project in Stevenage have an increased awareness and understanding of what equal opportunities means, and what barriers there are to achieving it, which is one of the major successes of TVEI. The issue has been put firmly on the agenda of many of our schools, and on the personal agendas of the people within them.

This has partly been achieved by the INSET that has been running, and this again has proved of great value and worth. The workshops and courses have crossed subject and professional divides, and in atmospheres of openness and supportiveness important areas have been explored. Significantly, for the last year of the project, several schools involved have identified equal opportunities as a key element in their own school-based TVEI INSET proposals, and internal working groups have been established. It is no longer a peripheral issue but one which has an important place in whole-school planning.

Other successes, in some or all of the schools, involve changes to the lower-school curriculum, to avoid different pupils receiving different curricula, and changes to option schemes which so often prove to bring about stereotyped choices. A place for topics based on equal opportunities has been found in many schools' social education programmes. These may seem piecemeal developments, but for a particular group of pupils within a school they can be significant. But many problems and barriers remain for us, and we are more aware of these for most of the time than of any successes. Until all the schools and those who manage them, including headteachers, take up equal opportunities as a live whole-school issue, and tackle it with determination, there will be only a small chance of a real breakthrough in attitudes and practice. We still have to transmit our own sense of awareness to our pupils, to their parents and of course to employers. We all know that changing attitudes is perhaps the most difficult aspect of any development but we have to find effective ways to do this if we are to take along with us, in our attempts to achieve greater equality of opportunity, the other groups to which we do have access. This may be daunting but it cannot be ducked.

As we write, the last year of the pilot scheme is now upon us, and we plan to continue some of our activities – the working group, the collection of data, the INSET, and the continuing debate of staffing policies – although we recognize that some aspects of the work are best now tackled at school level, with the continuing support of TVEI Project staff.

As we more towards the end of the pilot project and enter the extension phase we are putting some of the activities under GRIST arrangements. An interest group has been formed since the last day workshop, of those who want the opportunity to explore the issues further, and support for a full programme of discussions, workshops and resource sharing has been forthcoming from the LEA. We are determined to explore all avenues for support.

What is already quite clear though, is that those of us who have been made aware of the inequality of opportunity in our schools, for pupils and staff, are not going to abandon our concerns at the end of the project. TVEI has given us an opportunity to begin to approach the issue. The achievement of equal opportunities remains, for us, a major concern.

CHAPTER 3

Case Study: Equal Opportunities and the Sheffield Curriculum Development Initiative (LAPP) *

DARYL AGNEW, MARGARET BOOTH,
PATSY KANE AND ELEANOR LEITCH

Lower-Attaining Pupils Programme

The central aim of the Lower-Attaining Pupils' Programme (LAPP) was defined by Sir Keith Joseph as the development of a more effective education for those 14- to 16-year-olds for whom current examinations were not designed. The emphasis was to be on a more practical and relevant curriculum. Although LAPP was launched in 1983 in the same year as TVEI, it was with comparatively modest funding and publicity. Initially, 13 LEAs were funded by the DES for 3 years to pilot alternative curriculum strategies; 4 further LEAs received funding for pilot projects from 1985 to 1988. The pilot projects have varied considerably in their formulations of alternative curriculum strategies; some have focused more upon the development of opportunities for vocationally oriented studies, others upon the development of 'basic skills', and yet others upon the re-examination of the whole curricular experience for lower-attaining pupils.

---

* The views expressed in this chapter are those of the authors and do not necessarily reflect those of the LEA.

Introduction

In 1985, the DES approved a proposal from the Sheffield LEA for funding under the Lower-Attaining Pupils Programme (LAPP). The project, known as the Curriculum Development Initiative (CDI), is funded until the Summer of 1988, with partial funding likely to continue for some years after that. The initial DES guidelines relating to LAPP did not refer specifically to equal opportunities or to gender issues, and neither did Sheffield's submission to the DES for LAPP funding. The LEA would, however, consider that its broad policy statement would apply to CDI as it applies to other aspects of the Authority's work. The Sheffield City Council supports a policy of equality of opportunity. It has published a policy statement describing an Equal Opportunities Code of Practice and has an associated training programme for its employees.

The Education Department supports this policy and its document *A Curriculum Policy for Sheffield Schools* states:

> It is the responsibility of headteachers and staff, in conjunction with governing bodies, to . . . make explicit the provision for . . . equality of opportunity. . . . Statements about the curriculum in Sheffield schools should reflect the Authority's commitment to the alleviation of educational inequality; the promotion of equal opportunities; the development of anti-racist, multicultural education. . . .

The LEA employs an Advisory Teacher for Equal Opportunities (Gender), and she worked with members of the CDI team, and with the secondees, on a number of occasions during the first year of the project.

This chapter will describe the ways in which gender issues have been examined and sex equality promoted within the LAPP Project. (While we use the term 'equal opportunities' to encompass issues of race, gender, disability, class and special educational needs, the term 'gender' has been used in referring specifically to matters of sex equality.) We will focus particularly on those features of the Sheffield project which have provided distinctive opportunities for development within this area. These include the implementation and evaluation of the teacher secondment programme, the provision of time for school-based review and the planning and establishment of the project's equal opportunities group.

First, it will be necessary to spell out the project's philosophy and organization and describe the relationship between the CDI central team and the project schools, locating both within the wider context of the LEA's curriculum development programme. Against this background, the chapter will then describe how equal opportunities was identified as an issue in CDI and how this impacted on curriculum and staffing issues within the teacher secondment programme. A case study of a school in which sex equality became a high priority will highlight a variety of factors which have proved critical to successful development in this area, e.g. the importance of introducing an equal opportunities perspective to an innovation from its inception. This case study will also illustrate the range of gender issues to which classroom teachers can positively address themselves when they have an appropriate forum for curriculum development in this area. The school ethos and style of management have a crucial role to play in supporting this work, in recognizing progress that is made and enabling specific initiatives to inform whole-school approaches.

Background to the project's planning phase and first year

The Project Director took up his post in September 1985, and two Curriculum Development Officers (CDOs) joined the project in January 1986. Around this time negotiations with the LEA resulted in seven schools being designated as project schools. Three of the project schools are known as the Associate Schools, and they are specifically concerned with looking at alternative assessment approaches. The other four schools are known as the Core Schools. They are undertaking major curriculum review in conjunction with the project, and it is with these four core schools that this chapter is concerned.

The CDI core schools were chosen by the LEA because it was perceived that they had shared needs and interests which could be addressed through the LAP programme. They are the four secondary schools in Sheffield with the highest incidence of socio-economic disadvantage in their catchment areas. They are also the four schools which have the lowest number of public examination passes per student. Although these are crude measures, they indicate something of the problems of lower attainment faced by the schools. This information is not in any way intended as a criticism of the schools themselves. Indeed, each of the headteachers concerned was not only enthusiastic about being involved in the project, but all the schools were very aware of their students' needs and were actively involved in trying to meet them long before the inception of CDI.

The project's first year – the school year 1985–6 – was used as a planning year, 1986–7 thus being the first year of direct involvement in the schools. At the time of writing, therefore, the project is only at the half-way point of its second year of operation in the schools. In December 1985, when CDI was at the beginning of its planning phase, the Chief Education Officer of the Sheffield LEA launched a major development programme for the city's schools. This programme, called School-Focussed Secondment (SFS), centred on the CEO's belief that there was a need for radical curriculum change in Sheffield schools, and that teams of teachers seconded from schools, working in conjunction with their school management teams, the LEA advisory service and Sheffield's University and Polytechnic, should be the mechanism through which this change would be brought about.

CDI and SFS are in many senses interlinked. At a philosophical level, we would agree with the need for radical curriculum change, and the potential for bringing this about through teachers working within a supportive framework. The SFS programme meant that, in addition to the funding provided by the DES, each of the four CDI core schools was able to have seconded teachers working directly with the CDI team. Finally, through SFS, two university tutors were also allocated to work with the CDI secondees, an important opportunity for additional expertise to be gained.

From the outset, the CDI Project has been committed to a policy of negotiation with its schools; indeed, the schools in many senses are the project! It was also recognized from the outset that if the project was to have any lasting effect, the approaches used must ensure above all else that when funding ends, and CDI no longer formally exists, the work of the project must have become an intrinsic part of the schools, and be able to continue. The first stages of negotiation with the schools, in early 1985, involved the headteachers, the project director and the two CDOs. In March, the key planning and decision-making group of the project was formed. This group is known as the Central Team, and consists of the director, two CDOs, two university tutors and four school CDI co-ordinators, each an assistant headteacher. The teacher secondment programme has enabled 60 staff, 15 from each school, to be seconded. Each teacher has been seconded for one term in each of the three school years 1986, 1987 and 1988. These 60 teachers are central to the development process within their own schools, and also in developing links across the four schools.

The identification of equal opportunities as an issue in CDI and the secondment programme

The central team began the process of negotiating the detailed work of the project in March 1986. It was agreed that some of the work would focus on the individual schools, and the CDOs and university tutors were each attached to one of the four schools in order to facilitate this school-based work. In addition, the nature of the programme which was to be offered to the seconded teachers was discussed at length, and a structure was finally adopted for the autumn term of 1986.

The secondment programme structure arose as a result of the schools defining the issues which they saw as being central for them in developing their curricula. During April 1986, each school identified a number of key issues in terms of its development, and the co-ordinators presented this information at a central team meeting held in May. Five issues were independently identified by all the schools: management of change, assessment and accreditation, teaching and learning strategies, community development and multicultural and equal opportunities issues. The exact process by which each individual school identified the five issues probably varied, but generally the co-ordinators take issues from central team meetings to their school management teams. It is then the responsibility of each management team to decide to what extent consultation with other staff should occur on any particular issue. The extent to which consultation appeared to have taken place on the selection of key issues is discussed on p. 38. In terms of the project as a whole, however, equal opportunities issues were identified as being of central importance by the schools themselves from the outset.

The secondment programme structure was designed in such a way that all secondees would receive some input in each of the five areas of shared concern recorded above. The equal opportunities input, considering issues of race, gender, special educational need and disability, took the form of five half-day sessions at the university in term one, and one day per week for each of three weeks in terms two and three. In addition, four secondees in term one also opted for additional INSET on multicultural and anti-racist education. This programme constituted the only formal input on the equal opportunities theme within the first year secondment programme. Throughout the year, however, secondees worked together informally, linked with initiatives in their schools, and were involved in 'whole-school' development tasks.

It was felt that some discussion with secondees, headteachers and co-ordinators around the theme of equal opportunities issues might help us to evaluate not only the effectiveness of the formal input to the secondment programme, but the 'knock-on' effects which this might have had within and across schools. The results of such discussion would, we felt, also help to inform our future planning, not only in the area of equal opportunities, but possibly within the project as a whole. Therefore we planned a series of confidential interviews with staff at each of the core schools. In the 17 interviews we completed, four broad areas were explored: views about the equal opportunities input made during the secondment programme, equal opportunities work within the interviewee's own school, equal opportunities links across the four core schools and the CDI staffing structure.

Evaluation of initial equal opportunities developments

The interviews provided a great deal of useful data for the project, and also raised some important issues. A brief summary of the key points which emerged is given below.

- The secondees had not understood that the schools themselves had identified equal opportunities as one of the five key issues for consideration during the project. They had not perceived that a special importance had been attached to this area.
- Almost all the secondees who were actually interviewed indicated that equal opportunities issues were relatively low on their list of personal priorities, both in school and on secondment. This highlighted a mismatch between the initial stated importance of equal opportunities for the schools, and the individual interests of the teachers they seconded.
- The individual work of seven secondees (out of the total of 60 secondments) was in the area of equal opportunities. All this work focused on multicultural and anti-racist approaches, and six of the secondments were in one school. There were no individual

commissions related to gender issues. Of the whole-school tasks on which groups of secondees worked in relation to their own schools, one focused on equal opportunities issues in developing a lower-school curriculum structure, the subject of the case study below.

- During the first year of the project 41 of the 60 secondment terms were taken up by male teachers, and only 19 by women. For almost the whole year, the central team consisted of 8 men and 2 women. In addition, all four headteachers are male. The majority of those interviewed felt that the high proportion of males closely involved in the project could have had some effect on the relatively low priority afforded to equal opportunities issues, and especially gender issues.

Development and planning for the second year

A detailed paper was written for the headteachers and CDI co-ordinators in the schools as a result of the interview data, and this is in the process of being discussed by the headteachers and the central team. In addition, a CDI Equal Opportunities Group had been established. This includes secondees, two members of the central team and others involved with the schools who are interested and able to attend. At present the group is coming to terms with the various roles which it might be able to play, but is concentrating on information sharing and exchange and a consideration of the links between low attainment and equality of opportunity. In the first year of CDI work in the schools, the central team members worked mainly with seconded teachers. One strategy for increasing CDI involvement in equal opportunities issues, is to work directly with those staff in the schools who have a particular interest in the area. Three of the schools already have established equal opportunities groups, and central team members, through the CDI Equal Opportunities Group, are making links with these groups in order to support their work in the schools.

So far, this chapter has aimed to present a picture of equal opportunities within the CDI Project, highlighting some of the issues which have been raised, and the ways in which they have been responded to. The following case study is taken from one of the four schools where equal opportunities generally, and gender issues in particular, have been taken into consideration in the development of a new curriculum structure for year 2 students. This development was the main focus of CDI work in the school during 1986–7, and the innovation was implemented in September 1987. It illustrates the variety of issues identified and the progress that can be made if gender is prioritized as a development issue from the outset. For the purpose of this chapter, a pseudonym has been used for the school. We will call it East Bank School.

East Bank School: a case study of the Year 2 development programme

East Bank School is one of the four CDI core schools. It is a mixed comprehensive school with about 500 students and 60 staff. The catchment area lies in the inner city, and consists largely of two complexes of high-rise flats and two council estates. The catchment area has the highest incidence of socio-economic deprivation of any comprehensive school in the city and, as a result, extra resources are made available to the school under the City Council's Positive Action Programme. A new headteacher was appointed to the school at the beginning of the summer term in 1985, and he is perceived by the staff to be very concerned to promote equality of opportunity within the school.

During the interviews held with secondees in the school, one said:

> I think the head is certainly very keen to establish equal opportunities in the school . . . there's obviously a move to make sure that women and men are not in stereotyped roles for a start.

Another secondee said:

> In our school the head would certainly be in favour of promoting equal opportunities, and further to that a number of people in the senior management team would be promoting that and pushing that, and so would a number of people on the staff.

It is acknowledged, however, that there was a range of views among the secondees and the staff in the school:

> As you could guess, across the staff as a whole – and this is mirrored to some extent across secondees – there's a whole spectrum of opinions ranging from the fervently in favour to the fervently opposed, or if not fervently opposed, fervently suspicious!

The headteacher himself acknowledged the support he received from his management team and staff in the area of equal opportunities:

> I think there are a lot of people here who are genuinely committed to a good education for kids, and see equal opportunities, particularly in the gender area, as being crucial to our kids.

He was particularly appreciative of the contribution made by the woman assistant headteacher in the school – the only female member of the senior management team – who had been appointed shortly after himself:

> She has also raised that (equal opportunities) in people's awareness, and keeps me up to the mark . . .

Throughout the period of CDI involvement in the school, beginning in January 1986, equal opportunities issues have been discussed and debated, and this debate and discussion would certainly have occurred regardless of project involvement in the school. In October 1986 an equal opportunities group was formed and it met regularly and considered many different issues related to equality of opportunity within the school. Almost 50 per cent of the staff have taken part in some aspect of the group's activities. In May 1987, the development of equal opportunities work was the major item considered by the school's governing body at one of its termly meetings.

Thus, the CDI Project has developed in East Bank School in an atmosphere where equality of opportunity is seen to be an important issue and one which the school has been trying to address for some time.

Involvement in CDI

The school identified a focus for its involvement with the CDI Project relatively early in the planning phase. In response to an LEA request for information about 'Curriculum Plans' which was received in February 1986, the headteacher responded:

> The intention is to develop a coherent curriculum for all students, to begin with the new intake into Year Two in September 1987.

He also wrote in this preliminary document that a central consideration would be:

> . . . such issues as equal opportunities, anti-sexism, multi-cultural
> provision and special educational needs: they will all be considered.

The focus of the CDI Project, the development of a new curriculum
for the intake year of 1987, was thus given an equal opportunities
perspective from the outset.

During March and April 1986, each of the four core schools
selected the 15 staff who would be seconded to the CDI Project. The
schools used different strategies for selection, and in the case of East
Bank, interested staff wrote applications and were interviewed. The
selection criteria for appointments were discussed by the management team beforehand, and one of them was that there should be 'a
balance of the sexes'. Another criterion was that there should be a
'balance of salary scales'. Had the majority of secondees been senior
members of staff, women teachers would have automatically been
discriminated against.

Seven men and six women were eventually selected. Two of them
were seconded for two terms each in the first year, making a total of
15 secondment terms. East Bank was the only core school where a
male/female balance was achieved. The other three schools did not
use a male/female balance as one of their selection criteria, and in
each case men heavily outnumbered women in the secondment programme. Under the SFS programme, five new staff were appointed
to each school to replace the secondees. In the case of East Bank
School, three of these were women, all of whom exhibited a high
level of understanding of equal opportunities issues. Two of them
were later appointed to the year 2 team.

The new Year 2 curriculum and staffing structure

In the autumn term of 1986, the first five secondees (two women and
three men) began the process of discussion, planning and consultation with a view to designing a new curriculum structure for Year 2.
In October, a basic model was drawn up and put to the staff. It
proposed that the Year 2 students in September 1987 should have a
base of their own within the school, a team of teachers who would
spend a good deal of their week with them, and a new curriculum. In
the discussions with staff that followed, and the documents that

duced, equality of opportunity was frequently raised as an issue, both in terms of organization and curriculum content. By the end of the autumn term 1986, a model had been agreed within the school, and the team of Year 2 staff was about to be appointed. The second-ment programme allowed seconded teachers the time not only to reflect fully on the development of a new curriculum structure, but also allowed them to consult with all staff throughout the process, thus encouraging whole-school 'ownership' of the new Year 2 approach from the outset.

A total of 18 East Bank teachers applied to be members of the Year 2 team, and 8 were appointed. A balanced team was a central consideration. Four women and four men were appointed, and one man and one woman were made joint co-ordinators of the team. The aims of the Year 2 development had been broadly formulated within the school prior to the appointment of the team. The team itself clari-fied and amended these. One of the their initial ten aims was 'to create a new "curriculum" for the intake year 1987 which has the equality of all as its foundation stone'.

Equality of opportunity in the planning phase

Once they were appointed, the team took over the key planning role from the seconded teachers. Time was made available for the team to meet by a virtual re-write of the school timetable after Easter. This indicated the importance attached to the development by the school, and the favourable staffing ratio in the school through the Authority's Positive Action Programme certainly helped to facilitate this.

At an early stage in the planning phase, a woman member of the team produced a document highlighting the equal opportunities issues which the team should consider. This document was intro-duced as follows:

> It is the view of the Second Year Team, and the Equal Opportunities Planning Group, that an Equal Opportunities perspective should underpin the entire curriculum. It is, therefore, essential for the team to consider issues relating to Equal Opportunities at all stages of the planning process.
>
> An Equal Opportunities perspective constitutes, not only care for the full development of each individual child, irrespective of class, gender, race, physical and intellectual ability, but also care for the promotion of a more caring, just and open society.

The document then went on to outline the implications for planning under the headings 'Pastoral', 'Social' and 'Staffing', and raised more than 50 issues for the team's consideration. Among these were gender-related questions such as the possible inclusion of all-girl/all-boy groupings, the issue of equal teacher contact time for boys and girls, an awareness of the need to avoid gender bias in textbooks and other materials, equal access for boys and girls to all aspects of the curriculum, and an awareness of the need to avoid gender bias in staff roles within the team. Although most members of the team certainly felt that pressure of time meant that this document was not considered in as much detail as they would have liked, it served to raise awareness, to act as a checklist, and could be used as an evaluative tool in the future against which to measure progress.

Key issues for staff and students

During the planning phase a number of issues were identified as fundamental to the successful promotion of sex equality. A number of these issues – departmental staffing, roles of group tutors, female and male staff working together – are ones that have often been overlooked in the emphasis that has been given to equal opportunities 'curriculum' development. But the role models which teachers provide are one of the most powerful aspects of the 'hidden curriculum', as East Bank School demonstrated in the following areas.

THE STAFFING OF VISUAL AND CREATIVE STUDIES

For a proportion of the week, Year 2 students work in base with the Year 2 Team. At other times team members accompany the students to other specialist areas of the school, and Year 2 staff work with the students alongside the specialist area staff. The Visual and Creative Studies (VSC) area had previously been attempting to break down sex-stereotyping in its teaching patterns, particularly involving women teachers in the traditional 'boys craft' areas. In terms of the staffing of VCS for Year 2, a team member who was also a member of the VCS area said that 're-jigging' had had to take place to ensure that there was a male/female balance, even though that meant:

> . . . putting some teachers in a supporting role because they're not knowledgeable enough yet in that particular area to lead a session . . .

so that's an up-to-the-minute example of where gender issues have been taking priority.

GROUP TUTORS

The team has six 'full-time' members, plus two staff from the special needs area, who together make up a further whole member of staff. There are 84 students in Year 2. At the planning stage a discussion was held about how students should be organized into tutor groups. At first it seemed that a decision would be taken to have four tutor groups, with other team members supporting in different capacities. A team member then pointed out that there was an equal opportunities issue there, as the four designated form tutors were, in fact, also all the scale 1 teachers in the team. Subsequently, a decision was taken to have six tutor groups, which operated in three pairs. All the tutors would have equal status in that role, including the two joint co-ordinators, and the three paired groups would each have one male and one female tutor.

TEACHING PAIRED TUTOR GROUPS

Much of the teaching done in base involves two tutors working in one room with their two tutor groups. This approach promotes many of the advantages of team teaching, and also enables students to observe men and women teachers working together as equal partners in the classroom. This aspect of the pairing is seen as being very important by team members, and particularly that students should be aware of a situation where the male teacher does not automatically take the lead, or automatically be seen to be dealing with 'discipline problems'. The team is aiming to promote positive role models of women teachers, particularly for the girls in their groups.

EQUALITY OF TEAM MEMBERS

The emphasis on staff teamwork within the new Year 2 development was seen as essential from the very earliest discussions which were initiated by the seconded teachers in the autumn term of 1986. When appointments were made, the criteria stated clearly that the management team and governors would be looking to appoint a team of staff whom they felt would work well together, not simply a group of staff with individual potential. The team members themselves, throughout the planning phase, worked closely together, and particularly attempted to give all members an 'equal voice', and to share decision making. The roles of the joint co-ordinators were seen as being co-ordinating roles, rather than roles which afforded them higher status or more power than other members of the group. Although the joint co-ordinators were both appointed to their posts as scale 3 teachers, this reflected the responsibilities which they had previously had within the school. There were no financial incentives for either the co-ordinators or other staff when they applied for team membership.

STUDENTS WITH SPECIAL EDUCATIONAL NEEDS

In recognizing the importance of making sure that staffing structures and female and male roles reflected the school's commitment to equal opportunities, it was also important to ask the same questions about the ways in which students' learning and ways of working were organized. The previous policy of East Bank School had been to form a 'sheltered group' in each year to cater for students who needed the highest levels of special needs support. Students spent a good deal of their time in this group, and the rest in mainstream classes. The Year 2 team and special needs area, after much discussion, felt that it would be appropriate, and more in keeping with the overall aims of the new development, to integrate the students who would have formed the sheltered group and to support them within the mainstream. A sophisticated system of support and other strategies were developed to meet the needs of these students, and the special needs area was also involved in working with team staff to devise a programme of work in 'basic skills' which could be used by all students in the year who needed help with particular aspects of their work. A desire to provide equality of opportunity for all students, and particularly to avoid 'labelling' students as members of a 'sheltered group', played a large part in the decisions taken during the planning and organization of special needs input to the new development.

Planning into practice: the role of the evaluation group

The Year 2 initiative was implemented in September 1987, and at the time of writing has therefore been in operation for only one and a half terms. It would clearly be inappropriate at this time to make any judgements on the success or otherwise of the team's attempt to introduce an equal opportunities perspective to their work. It is, however, possible to give some tentative first impressions.

The team member who had compiled the original equal opportunities document during the planning stage expressed some concern about an overview:

> I feel that the equal opportunities issue is worrying me at the moment, not because nothing is happening, but because I feel we ought to be keeping track of things more as we go through, rather than it being ad hoc. . . . If we don't monitor those things and we don't actually share with the rest of the staff developments which have been made, and which appear to be positive, it's going to be like an isolated outpost.

On the other hand, she felt that the central advantage for the present was that all members of the team were 'aware of the issues', that 'à lot of progress had been made on that basis', and more would be made in the future. In this respect the role of the evaluative group was an important means of ascertaining future direction but also signalling past achievements to those who have been initiating developments in this area.

It had been the intention of the management team of East Bank School that the Year 2 development should be evaluated, and in consultation with them and the Year 2 team, the school's CDI tutor had written a document about the basic philosophy which should be applied during the evaluation. During the first half of the autumn term an Evaluation Co-ordination Group, chaired by the CDI tutor, and consisting of members of the Year 2 team, management team and other staff, was established. This group negotiated strategies for what was agreed to be the 'first phase' of evaluation with the Year 2 team. Ten hours of directed time were made available to each member of the group to carry out their evaluative role. The CDI tutor was able to spend a much greater length of time co-ordinating the work of the group, and drafting the documents, a commitment which would have been difficult to meet from within school hours alone. The evaluation work was, however, another example of how time was made available through CDI and the school which provided teachers with the opportunity to take on a new role, and to learn new skills which could be applied later to other in-school situations.

During the 2 weeks immediately before the October half-term holiday, members of the evaluation co-ordination group undertook a series of lesson observations and also interviewed Year 2 staff and students. The aim of the exercise was to build up a picture of 'first impressions', to emphasize positive aspects of the process to date, and to raise issues for further consideration. This phase of the evaluation was intentionally very broad, and no specific emphasis was placed on evaluating the success of equal opportunities approaches, or any other specific aspect of the work. Nevertheless, a number of equal opportunities issues did arise during this first phase, and these will be considered briefly below.

Issues identified through evaluation

KNOWING THE STUDENTS

One of the most positive indicators to emerge from the first phase of the evaluation was the high level of satisfaction expressed by staff and students about staff/student relationships. Much of this centred around the perceptions of team members that they knew the students in their tutor groups very well:

> At this stage I feel quite confident to answer questions on each kid about their academic ability, personality traits, what they have diffi- culty with, what they're good at, to a certain extent home background . . . really, details which I think would have taken a full year before.

Team members saw many advantages in 'knowing' their students so well:

> We pick up very fast on their behaviour or if they're having learning difficulties, and we're able to transmit that information round much faster than we used to be able to.

There was a feeling that the team/base structure was enabling staff to know, understand and work with individuals, and to meet their individual needs – a key issue in any aim to achieve equality of opportunity.

STUDENTS WITH SPECIAL EDUCATIONAL NEEDS

Team members were very positive about the new arrangements for students with special needs, and the classroom observation exercise supported this view. Team teaching in base was proving to be very successful, and the technique was often employed whereby one teacher paid particular attention to the students who needed most support, while the other made a less intensive input among other students. There was also evidence that more able students were supporting less able students in working situations. A small 'multi-sensory' group was providing individual support for six students in the year who had the most severe learning difficulties. One team member said: 'They love going to the multi-sensory group. Their friends want to go with them!'

One of the teachers from the special needs area who was also a member of the Year 2 team summed up her feelings after the first half-term as follows:

> We've tried to provide for the [special needs] kids in a different way, and that's the most rewarding thing . . . I find it very challenging to work with staff and 'skill' staff up to dealing with special needs – rather than to go in there and firefight yourself, which is what we tend to do around the school.

THE PAIRED TUTOR RELATIONSHIP

On the whole the paired tutor relationship was working well, and team members identified many advantages both for themselves and for their students. There was a general feeling that roles were being equally shared within the classroom, that they were taking turns to lead and support in lessons, and that positive relationships between staff were encouraging positive relationships between students in the classroom. On the whole, the partnerships were felt to be equal, although one of the women said, with some resignation: 'I do worry that their [the students'] perceptions are still that he is in charge!'

EQUALITY OF TEAM MEMBERS

The team members were all aware that it had proved very difficult to put their ideal democratic model of operation into practice in circumstances when they were under pressure to make decisions and were very short of time to do so:

> We were going to be ever so democratic and make whole-team decisions, and that, I feel, over a period of time, became more difficult. We're still aiming at it, but there's so much to decide upon, and so much to do.

The co-ordinators were felt to be in a particularly difficult position because they were negotiating on behalf of the team with members of the management team and other staff. They had, at times, taken decisions which other members of the team had not participated in, and this had caused some feelings of dissatisfaction, that corporate decision making was not occurring. One particular issue which, again, seemed to be largely related to pressure of time, was that the co-ordinators' roles had themselves become differentiated, and that the male co-ordinator was tending to fulfil a 'curriculum' role, as a result of his past experience, whereas the woman was taking on the 'pastoral' role as a result of hers. There was concern among the team about this traditional sex-stereotyping, but also a sense of resignation – that in the circumstances it was almost inevitable.

The team members were well aware of all the issues raised above, and were actively seeking to maintain their ideal model of working by discussing them and seeking ways forward.

GENDER ISSUES IN THE CLASSROOM

The observation exercise indicated that both working patterns and relationships in the classroom were very positive. Several instances were noted, however, when boys were dominating the classroom situation, whereas no instances were recorded of girls dominating in a similar way. One observer noted: 'A certain group of boys had the teacher all to themselves.' During another activity: 'A certain group of boys got all the teacher's attention.' And in another situation, where students were doing an activity in turn: 'The boys all went first, and then the girls.'

In another lesson a teacher played a game with students for the last few minutes. Five boys had a turn. The teacher said 'it's the girls' turn now'. One girl had a turn and then the bell went for the end of the lesson.

Almost all these incidents occurred in lessons which were out of base, and were being taught by Area rather than team staff, but there is clearly an equal opportunities issue here which needs to be addressed.

Conclusion

The CDI Project in Sheffield has more than half of its time yet to run, and this chapter is therefore recording a process to date, rather than offering any overall analysis or any summative account of the treatment of equal opportunity or gender issues.

The philosophy of the project is based on the principle of negotiation, evaluation and change. Our structures are not predetermined by any outside agency and, as the project advances, we would see that where evaluation of those structures leads to adaptation and change, this is indicative of one of our key strengths, rather than a weakness.

A consideration of equal opportunities issues within the project to date reflects this process well. In the first year of the programme an approach was adopted which proved to have several limitations. In the light of these, new approaches have been negotiated, and these themselves will also be evaluated and adapted in the future.

In some senses the Year 2 development at East Bank School, and the equal opportunities perspective included in it, is a microcosm of the project approach. Certain strategies have been planned by the team, the extent of their success is, even at this early stage, being considered; and attempts are already being made to adapt and improve some aspects of the work.

Perhaps three other issues worthy of note are highlighted in this chapter. The first is that both in terms of the project as a whole, and the Year 2 development in particular, it is clear that issues related to equality of opportunity can be addressed and progress can be made when individual teachers and members of management teams make these a priority in the day-to-day working of their schools. Conversely, it is very difficult to make progress when issues relating to equality of opportunity are marginalized, or lack of interest is shown by the school as a whole, or by individuals within it.

Secondly, the example of the East Bank Year 2 development seems to indicate the advantages to be gained in being able to introduce an equal opportunities perspective to an innovation from its inception. It is very much more difficult to graft a consideration of these issues on to a system or organization which has developed without such a perspective, and already exhibits in-built discrimination as a result. Such is the case in many aspects of the present education system.

Finally, the CDI programme, through secondment, offers teachers the opportunity to become actively involved in all phases of innovative work within their schools: planning, consultation, implementation and evaluation. The schools themselves, having recognized the importance of providing time and space for teachers to think, plan and act, have developed strategies for involving many other staff in the process. As a result, change and development has occurred in each of the schools well beyond that which might normally have been feasible. In East Bank School particularly, an increase in awareness about the importance of equality of opportunity for both students and staff has occurred, and efforts to put the awareness into practice will certainly continue in the future.

CHAPTER 4

Case Study: Issues of Gender in the Inner London Education Authority Profile and London Record of Achievement Scheme*

JACKIE KEARNS

Records of Achievement

The aim of the Records of Achievement initiative was to explore the implications of a record of achievement for 16-year-olds and to provide a basis for the development of national guidelines for the introduction of these records for all such pupils from 1990. The Department of Education and Science saw the benefits of the development of such records in terms of improved student motivation, more careful identification of individual student needs, an acknowledgement of their achievements and a final record which would be valued and recognized by employers.

The pilot projects began in 1985 and were funded initially for 3 years with extension funding already planned for a further 2 years. Twenty-two LEAs, either working independently or cooperating with other LEAs, were involved in nine pilot projects. The number of schools involved in each LEA has varied from project to project. Unlike TVEI and LAPP, however, which initially involved discrete groups of students in their schools, Records of Achievement developments have been directed at all students in the school cohorts and have therefore involved a larger number of teachers.

---

* The views expressed in this chapter are those of the author and do not necessarily reflect those of the LEA.

The Profile and London Record of Achievement Pilot Scheme was one of nine schemes that took part in a national pilot of Records of Achievement funded by the Department of Education and Science in 1985–8. The Pilot Scheme was one of several that received extended funding for the period 1988–90.

In this chapter the principles that underlay the work of the Profile and London Record of Achievement Pilot Scheme and its organization in the period 1985–8 are described and the issues in using these principles and profiling practice to combat gender stereotyping are explored. Finally, the kinds of gender stereotyping that the initial work of the Pilot Scheme identified are examined.

The London Record of Achievement

It is the policy of the Inner London Education Authority (ILEA) that by 1990 every student of school-leaving age shall compile a portfolio that provides evidence of their positive achievements during their school years, a London Record of Achievement. The portfolio provides a common framework, which is recognized by those offering employment, further education or training to students. The four elements of the London Record of Achievement are:

1 A student statement in which students describe their achievements both inside and outside school and reflect positively on their personal and social skills, as well as their particular interests and aspirations.
2 A school statement in which teachers give a positive picture of the achievements of their students.
3 Samples or photographs of good pieces of work.
4 Certificates gained in competitive and non-competitive examinations and tests, including awards received inside and outside school, summary subject profiles, unit credits, graded assessments and public examination certificates.

The London Record of Achievement portfolio belongs to the student, who writes the student statement and selects the samples of work and certificates for inclusion in it.

The compilation of the London Record of Achievement portfolio is based on the new forms of assessment that provide descriptive evidence of the positive achievements of students throughout their period of compulsory education; these are being developed throughout the country, as well as in the ILEA. These forms of descriptive assessment are usually referred to as profiles and, although there are almost as many different interpretations of profiling as people using this kind of assessment, the words profile and profiling are used in this chapter as a generic term for the different forms of descriptive assessment. Although developments in profiling are well established in further and higher education and are spreading into primary schools, the focus here is the experience of the ILEA Pilot Scheme in the secondary phase.

Organization of the Pilot Scheme

In the second half of the autumn term 1985 and the spring term 1986 teachers in 18 secondary schools and two special schools in the ILEA started work on developing profiles and records of the achievements of their students as part of the Profile and London Record of Achievement Pilot Scheme, which was 70 per cent funded by an Education Support Grant until March 1988. In the course of the project 58 further secondary schools, 9 special schools and 16 off-site centres joined the Pilot Scheme and work commenced in several colleges of further education. This meant that more than half the Authority's institutions with students in the 11–19 age range were involved in the scheme from September 1987 in preparation for the implementation of the London Record of Achievement across the whole of the ILEA from September 1988.

The development work undertaken in the pilot schools was supported by a central team of seconded teachers who spent 1 day a week working with teachers and students in each institution. Development work was co-ordinated in schools by a profiling co-ordinator, who was almost without exception a member of the senior management team and, therefore, in a position to support the implementation of a whole-school policy on assessment and to relate it to the school's policies on equality of opportunity.

The development officers were so named because their role was seen as supporting teachers in working from their own particular starting points in developing ways of describing and then raising the achievements of their students. The development officers were not importing a ready-made package of practice in assessment into schools, but rather aimed to work within the ethos of the school.

It was recognized that in seeking to change the way they work with their students, teachers make themselves vulnerable and need time, space and support to develop and test their ideas. In this process the model of the outside expert has limitations and the decision to appoint classroom practitioners as development officers proved its worth, as they understood the pressures under which their colleagues worked and identified with them. Their status as colleagues made it possible for them to offer support as equals and to share developing expertise between teachers in the same and different schools. Their role was that of facilitators and communicators in the process of development and change. This involved not only discussions with colleagues in order to share, develop and clarify ideas, but support in preparing papers, materials and assessment formats and in organizing and running meetings and providing feedback at all levels of a school's organization. The expertise of the development officers developed with that of their colleagues in schools and was, therefore, founded in concrete practice. There was in essence only one question: how can profiling support the development and progress of students? The answers led teachers to review what they were teaching and how they were teaching it.

The way in which the Pilot Scheme sought to address equal opportunities further illustrates the project's philosophy. Initially, the Pilot Scheme's liaison officer, who had expertise in the area of equal opportunities, was given responsibility for this aspect of the work of the team. After a few months the liaison officer, with the support of the team, changed her role to that of a development officer working in schools, while maintaining her specific interest in equal opportunities. This aspect of the work was then integrated into every team member's responsibilities, a strategy which was made easier to implement because from the outset each member of the team was committed to developing and implementing policy on equality of opportunity. Exploration of issues in relation to equality of opportunity takes place in the team through a standing committee and frequent whole-team discussions, as well as through evaluating experience in schools and providing inservice support for teachers with regard to equal opportunities and issues in assessment.

When the Pilot Scheme expanded, new development officers were sought who would be able to discuss in depth issues relating to equality of opportunity and assessment. Those who approached assessment from the starting point of the needs of students and who perceived a need for students to take control of their own learning were most likely to be appointed as development officers. They were also those most likely to understand the philosophy of the project and the principles that had developed from the initial work of the teachers in the pilot schools with their development officer colleagues.

Consideration of equal opportunities issues had, therefore, a clear place within the work of the project team. This aspect of the project team's work took place within the context of the ILEA's stated concern to enhance the quality of education of all students, regardless of class, sex, race or previous level of achievement.

Principles

Some of the ideas that motivated the work of the teachers in the pilot schools were:

1 A desire to accentuate the strengths of their students and so help them gain the self-confidence to overcome difficulties and achieve more.
2 A belief that students make better progress when they understand from the outset the aims and objectives of their courses and the basis on which their work is being assessed.
3 A belief that when students and their families have a clear picture of the demands being made of them at school, then students are in a better position to take responsibility for and discuss their own learning and to become self-motivated.
4 A recognition of the importance of valuing the social and personal skills that students have and those they develop and demonstrate in the course of their learning.
5 A realization that comments on the progress made by students are most meaningful when they are made in the context in which learning has taken place and relate to specific aspects of learning.

These ideas developed within the context of a growing understanding of the central role of assessment not only in the stated curriculum but, more powerfully, in the hidden curriculum of schools. It is not only what is assessed that defines for students what really matters at school, but the way that assessment takes place. For example, discussion and cooperative approaches may play a large part in the organization of learning, but if work is assessed and credit given on an individual basis in written tests and students are in competition with one another, then they receive contradictory messages about what really matters in the curriculum. This may explain the frustration some teachers experience when their efforts to provide more stimulating approaches to learning are rejected by students, who demand to be prepared for the examinations and tests on which they know they will be judged.

The development of profiles of the achievements of secondary age students in the ILEA has taken place in the dual context of a desire to enhance the quality of education of all students, regardless of class, sex, race or previous level of achievement, and a broader definition of what constitutes achievement than is traditionally assessed in public examinations. This definition of achievement extends beyond the acquisition and re-presentation of knowledge required in public examinations to the application of knowledge, for example in solving problems, and the personal and social skills that support learning. This wider definition of achievement makes it possible to accentuate the positive attributes of young people that do not necessarily reflect the narrow demands of the public examination system or tests of ability in the cognitive area alone.

In devising profiling schemes that reflect this broader definition of achievement and that support learning, many teachers have devised their own course planning sheets in order to set out clearly the aims, objectives, content and structure of courses, information that is then shared with students and their parents and families.

Profiling formats vary from school to school, but there are many common features. Most profiles are headed by a description of the content of the course or unit of work and give information on learning aims and objectives. This provides a context for the comments made by teachers and students. The comments of teachers are usually given under headings. These are often subject-specific, but may be cross-curricular or relate to the broader definition of achievement described above. The comments made by students on their own work may be under headings or be unstructured. The student self-assessment is usually the place where future targets for improving work are given. The whole profile provides a basis for discussion between students and their teachers, parents and families.

This open, descriptive approach to profiling emphasizes how important it is that profiles of the achievements of students reflect the context in which the learning has taken place. This is in sharp contrast to profiles based upon statement banks and checklists of skills that are often produced centrally in order to form the basis of nationally validated profiling schemes, which impose their own

cultural values on students and teachers. The attraction of such
centrally produced schemes is that they appear to offer a way of
comparing students, based on validating that they can do or have
achieved the skills described in the statements. However, the reader
of the checklist has no knowledge of the actual work undertaken to
'achieve' the statements, and there is often a form of collusion
between teachers and students to 'do' the work to 'get' the statements, without the student developing more than a superficial
understanding of the work involved or developing ownership of it.
These are the reasons for the oft-heard criticism of such centrally
determined profiles that are based on pre-written statements that the
assessments are meaningless.

The approach to profiling based upon the principles outlined in
this section has implications for how all students perceive school.
The next section will explore some of these in relation to the opportunities profiling can provide for enhancing the way girls experience
the curriculum.

The potential of profiling for female students

While it is the intention to focus here on profiling in relation to girls,
it is clear that open, descriptive forms of assessment have the potential for improving the way all students experience the curriculum of
schools.

Traditionally, developments in assessment have focused on
finding the most accurate ways of measuring performance and
ranking students accordingly. Assessments have taken the form of
end-of-course examinations that are not part of the learning and that
do not allow students to return and improve their performance in the
light of lessons learned from taking the examination.

In contrast, the open, descriptive approach to assessment focuses
on the process of learning being engaged in by individual students
and does not support competition between them for the allocation of
grades or marks. Rather, students consider their strengths and weaknesses in relation to the work they are engaged in and apply the
lessons they have learned to the next area of work, building on
strengths and aiming to overcome weaknesses. This form of assessment makes comparisons between students redundant. The
compilation of the London Record of Achievement portfolio at the
end of compulsory schooling enables students to provide a summary

of achievements throughout their time at school and a positive description of the way they approach their learning, as well as concrete examples of good pieces of work and certificated evidence of achievement. An evaluation of the first portfolios produced in the summer term 1987 showed that girls are significantly more successful than boys at compiling examples of good work and certificates and other evidence of their achievements. This positive approach of using assessment to support the way students learn combats the poor self-image and passivity that are often created in girls and working-class students by negative, competitive forms of assessment.

The experience of teachers in the Pilot Scheme suggests that the format of profiles is a very important factor in the way language is able to be used. Girls usually respond well to the opportunity provided by open formats to write freely and discursively about their work and enjoy discussing their profiles with their peers and their teachers. Boys may experience greater difficulties in expressing themselves freely and often prefer a more closed format, where, for example, they choose between pre-written sentences in order to identify their skills.

Girls commonly allow their abilities and achievements to go unrecognized and even deprecate them. The positive cooperative approach to describing a student's achievements makes it possible to enhance the self-image of girls and helps them to take charge of the progress of their own learning, as they reflect on the way they learn best and set themselves targets for future ways of working. It can provide an antidote to the negative and unsubtle effects of labelling students by the use of grades.

By helping girls, particularly working-class girls, to appreciate what they have achieved and can achieve, it is possible to create an expectation of success that normally is the preserve of middle-class students. Because they are part of the dominant culture, middle-class students, and middle-class boys in particular, often develop an unthinking acceptance of the way the teacher, who is also part of the dominant culture, presents abstract knowledge. In supporting girls and working-class students in valuing their achievements and taking control of the progress of their own learning, it is important to understand that they may phrase their ideas and questions in a way that does not conform to the teaching style. In exploring these with them, it is therefore necessary to appreciate that they may be trying to come to terms with a contradiction between the abstract concepts with which they are being presented and their own concrete experience. The open, cooperative approach to assessment encourages a teaching style that takes all students' modes of expression seriously and makes time to explore their questions and ideas supportively with them. At the same time, by making learning aims explicit and discussing them and the basis for assessments with students, it becomes possible for students to acquire the language of assessment that has so long been the preserve of teachers and examiners. Profiling, by fostering individual support and discussion, makes it possible to realize the aim of enabling students to formulate their own hypotheses and questions, as well as having them posed for them by their teachers.

A cooperative approach to assessing the work of students gives greater scope for the development and recognition of the facilitative skills that are often regarded as *female* attributes than the competitive and *male* skills that have traditionally been fostered in a system that has been based on making comparisons between students. The focus is on fostering the development of individual students in relation to their own work and potential, not on how well or badly they are able to stand up to competition with peers.

The experience of teachers generally that, when girls engage in practical work they usually prefer to read and plan before starting, while boys normally want to get straight into action, can be exploited to the benefit of girls in the way profiling involves making learning aims and objectives explicit to students at the beginning of a course or unit of work. However, in making explicit the aims and objectives of a course or unit of work, it is important to remember that when students take control of their own learning, they will necessarily raise questions and develop ideas that do not fit in with the way the teaching had been planned.

When learning aims and objectives and assessment criteria are established, it is necessary to keep in mind the uneven nature of the process of acquiring knowledge and developing skills. This militates against a too rigid predetermining of the outcomes of learning. Similarly, the setting of targets for the future should emerge from self-assessment and discussion of the work of individual students rather than from general objectives that have been predetermined for the group at the beginning of the course.

The potential of using open, cooperative forms of assessment like profiling in the form it is described here to enhance the way girls experience the curriculum is considerable. However, profiling of itself does not necessarily change relationships in the classroom. The work of the Pilot Scheme showed that what an examination of written profiles and self-assessments and the review discussions that are a part of the process of profiling can reveal, is how gender and other forms of stereotyping are taking place and, therefore, provide teachers with evidence on which to take remedial action.

Experience of gender stereotyping in developing profiles of the achievements of students

The final section of this chapter draws on the experience of the Pilot Scheme to examine some of the implications of gender stereotyping. It also identifies some aspects of profiling where teachers will wish to be particularly sensitive.

Profiling the personal and social skills of students is particularly problematic. In the ILEA Pilot Scheme a distinction is made between the profiling of *personal and social skills* that students demonstrate as part of their approaches to learning and the making of unsubstantiated and necessarily subjective comments on the *innate personal qualities* of students. This distinction is a crucial one if prejudice is to be avoided. It is, however, very difficult to operate in practice, particularly given the subjective nature of all assessment.

For girls the approach taken to profiling personal and social skills is particularly important because, as the experience of the Pilot Scheme shows, girls are far more likely than boys to receive comments on their profiles on the way they interact socially. The achievements of girls tend to be seen in the context of their social expertise, those of boys in terms of getting the task done. This emphasis is reflected in self-assessments made by girls. An evaluation of the very first London Record of Achievement portfolios produced in the summer term 1987 showed, for example, that girls were significantly more likely to include details of charity work and family responsibilities than boys. It also showed that in those cases where teachers predicted the future career potential of students, 70 per cent of the comments related to boys and only 30 per cent to girls.

Girls are praised for being friendly, helpful and compliant and suffer from positively intended stereotyping (*a nice, quiet member of the group*) more than from consciously negative comments. Such comments on the personal qualities of students are not appropriate in a profile of the social and personal skills that relate to a student's learning and, indeed, are less frequently found in profiles of the achievements of boys.

When comments are made on the social and personal skills that support learning, there is a tendency to focus on those that reinforce a passive role for girls. Girls receive comments on their ability to listen and on the neatness and presentation of their work to a significantly greater degree than boys. When weaknesses have to be overcome, boys are more likely to receive positive injunctions to *apply themselves more* or to seek to *extend their concentration span*, whereas girls are told to *waste less time or chat less*. When perceived negatively, girls' talk in class may be characterized as *idle chatter*, whereas boys' talk is described as a *lively exchange of ideas*. Ironically, girls may subsequently be criticized for lacking confidence; that is exhorted to improve, when the opportunities for that improvement have been reduced.

While the arguments for giving girls access to all subjects in the curriculum are well rehearsed, the experience of the Pilot Scheme shows that once girls have gained access to such subjects as the physical sciences, it is vital to monitor that underachievement is not accepted as the norm for them in these areas. Low expectations of girls in some subjects can be identified by comparing their profiles with those of boys to see whether comments made by teachers accept underachievement and whether there is evidence that self-assessment is taken less seriously by girls in these subjects. An under-expectation of achievement by girls may also be reflected in the targets that they set themselves for future work in discussion with their teachers.

Self-assessment can lead to supportive discussions between girls and their teachers about the factors to which they attribute *successes* and *failures* and the strategies they need to develop to improve the way they work and learn. Such discussions place a heavy burden of insight upon teachers, a burden for which, as yet, there has been little staff development work. (Indeed, inservice support for the conducting of review sessions with students has been one of the most frequently named priorities of teachers working on developing profiling.) Not only can self-assessment reflect stereotyping that has been internalized by girls, but it can also lead to discussions in which stereotyped self-images are reinforced. Furthermore, when preparing guidelines for students to support them in writing self-assessments, it is easy to invite students to comment on active, competitive areas of their experience rather than to focus equally on reflective or apparently more passive aspects. This could disadvantage girls in relation to their male peers.

Not the least of the dangers of review sessions based on profiles and self-assessments is that of the articulate teacher dominating the discussion while the student merely assents. This is a particular problem for girls, who, experience shows, are much less likely than boys to contest the assessments made of their work and who are more likely to undervalue their achievements. Some schools are considering enabling students to choose the teacher with whom they discuss the statement they write for their London Record of Achievement portfolio. This would enable girls to choose to work with a female teacher.

Peer group discussions can be supportive, with students helping one another to recognize strengths and give credit to achievements, but girls often fear to stand out from the crowd, to be seen as pushy or over-confident. This leads them to understate their achievements and can be destructive, particularly in a mixed classroom. For girls in some cultural groups it is seen as a negative attribute to talk about one's strengths and achievements. For these reasons it is often better for girls to discuss in pairs and, in any event, the teacher has to plan carefully to create an environment of solidarity between students, as well as being prepared to step in and offer support where necessary.

Experience has shown that for the girls and their families whose first language is not English, preparing the student statement in their mother tongue has been a significant and positive experience. Making the translation into English that accompanies the original statement in the London Record of Achievement portfolio is not a mechanical exercise and it is best done by the student herself in discussion with peers, bilingual adults or teachers who have some understanding of translating between languages. If the student statement is typed in English, then it should also be typed in the mother tongue, as long as to do this does not culturally devalue the handwritten script. Where no written form of the mother tongue exists, some schools are exploring the use of taped statements.

As this section has revealed, there are many ways in which gender stereotyping may feature within the assessment and profiling process. In order to maximize the chances of such stereotyping being reduced, teachers will need to be alerted to these issues and encouraged to develop strategies for tackling the problem.

Conclusions

Profiling as it has been developed within the Profile and London Record of Achievement Pilot Scheme has provided teachers with a tool with which to monitor their own work on assessment in terms of its implications for equality of opportunity. The existence of a central team of development officers committed to the promotion of equality of opportunity, working within an LEA with a high level of commitment to equal opportunities, has made it possible for many issues to be discussed and various strategies for overcoming problems to be explored.

It is clear from the examination of the issues as presented in this chapter that profiling systems have to be part of an assessment policy for the school that is consonant with policies on equality of opportunity. This policy will have to recognize the contradiction between competitive systems of assessment, which no school can evade, and the open, cooperative approach to assessment described here, an approach that makes it possible not only to identify where gender stereotyping is taking place, but provides a vehicle for enabling girls to develop the confidence and strategies they need if they are to take control of their own learning. By taking control of their own learning girls are acquiring skills that can help them to take control of their own lives.

CHAPTER 5

Case Study: Tameside and Rochdale Equal Opportunities Project (TRIST) *

HILARY ANSLOW AND DAVID DICKINSON

TVEI-Related Inservice Training

TVEI-Related Inservice Training (TRIST) was introduced as an inservice training scheme to promote developments across the curriculum of the kind related particularly to TVEI. TVEI's equal opportunities criterion therefore had significance for this inservice training project. The national TRIST initiative was funded by the MSC and its projects ran between September 1985 and April 1987. LEAs in receipt of funds for these short-term projects were charged with basing their arrangements on a systematic assessment of inservice needs in relation to future curriculum development plans. Through the projects, LEAs were able to set up INSET activities and finance supply cover for teachers engaged in them. The ways in which schools were involved in this programme varied significantly between LEAs. It was intended that lessons learnt from the TRIST pilot projects should be the foundation of LEA planning for the Grant-Related Inservice Training (GRIST) programme which commenced in 1987.

Introduction

In April 1986 the Rochdale and Tameside Local Education Authorities received £75,000 from the Manpower Services Commission

---

* The views expressed in this chapter are those of the authors and do not necessarily reflect those of the LEAs.

(MSC) for TVEI Related Inservice Training (TRIST) to reduce gender inequalities in the secondary curriculum. The TREO (Tameside and Rochdale Equal Opportunities) project was born. The joint LEA submission asked for funding for two full-time project officers at deputy headteacher (Group 11) level, accountable to a TREO Management Group consisting of officer, adviser and teacher representatives from both LEAs, as well as TVEI and MSC representatives. The work began in earnest when the project officers took up their posts at the beginning of June 1986. By March 1987 the following had attended workshops across the two LEAs: 47 headteachers, 45 deputy headteachers, 13 advisers, 2 deputy directors, 9 education officers, 2 TVEI co-ordinators, 2 educational psychologists, 1 FE director, 1 Theatre-in-Education Liaison Officer, 2 heads of Careers Service, 29 Middle managers and 53 Curriculum Working Group representatives.

In addition, there were 11 school-based INSET sessions and a school governors' workshop. Action plans to reduce gender inequalities had been produced by 54 middle and secondary schools/colleges and each institution received copies of booklets produced by the curriculum working groups.

This 1-year pilot project was organized in three carefully structured phases:

1 The first phase gave training to headteachers, advisers and education officers. The headteachers were asked to complete a pre-workshop task which focused on issues of gender for students and staff within their own institutions. At the end of the workshop they recorded a series of action points for their own school/college.
2 The second phase provided training for a deputy from each institution whose pre-workshop task was to ask the headteacher/principal about the action points s/he had recorded for the school/college and then to look at aspects of the school's working environment which might help or hinder implementation. At the end of their own training course, deputies were asked to record strategies for implementation.
3 For the third phase the emphasis in each LEA was different with Tameside providing training for middle management and Rochdale forming nine curriculum working groups to examine teaching processes and materials. Middle managers with responsibility for option choices attended a 5-day course. Their pre-

workshop task was to talk to the deputy and analyse materials relating to option choices. Each curriculum working group produced a booklet of recommendations which was sent to all special, middle and secondary schools to be used in the context of school-based INSET work. In addition, in-service training sessions for some school staff and governors were led by the two project officers.

A year later in March 1987 the MSC agreed to fund with £25 000 a fourth phase to run until August 1987. This phase was for dissemination of the project locally, regionally and nationally. As part of the local dissemination, workshops were held for primary headteachers. At these workshops emphasis was placed on awareness raising, the development of positive attitudes towards equal opportunities and their expression in curriculum planning and organization. A copy of the ILEA's Primary Matters (1986) was distributed to every school. In addition the TREO project has been disseminated to TVEI networks regionally and nationally. A booklet (North-West TRIST 1987) written by the two project officers to outline the TREO strategy has been sent to every LEA.

In this chapter, the context and origins of the project, and the role of the MSC as the sponsoring agency, will be examined, the TREO training model and strategy will be described, and there will be an attempt to identify and evaluate the key factors in the development of the project. Finally, possible future developments will be identified. It must be stressed that the views expressed are the personal ones of the project officers informed by their work for the project, by the formal evaluation of an external evaluator, the informal evaluation of the management group, and the teachers who participated.

The origins and context of the project

Both LEAs are small, nestling in the foothills of the Pennines as part of the Greater Manchester conurbation, and both have a sizeable minority of students of South Asian Muslim background. The successful submission for TRIST money was eventually written by a female general adviser in the Rochdale LEA and a male Deputy Director of Education in the Tameside LEA; the link between the LEAs had been established through the Women in Education network. Very little work on gender, initiated by the LEA, had taken place in Rochdale. Although Tameside had been making advances through its involvement with the Girls Into Science and Technology Project, little had been done in other subject areas or on a whole-school basis. A gender breakdown of staffing figures in both LEAs clearly demonstrated an imbalance at middle management and senior management levels. However, in various schools in both LEAs, committed individuals were working on gender in the class-room and occasionally in the staffroom.

Project aims and strategy

The aims of the project as detailed in the submission to the MSC were:

- to work in partnership across the two LEAs giving priority to work on gender equality;
- to give training in gender equality to school and LEA managers;
- to build an atmosphere of understanding and support for the issue among senior managers and give them responsibility for action; and
- to initiate and develop action within each LEA and its schools.

The MSC had not approved a proposal in the original submission to raise the awareness of school governors, parents and employers, and therefore the concentration was to be upon teachers. Neither was the development of anti-sexist student resources and, therefore, the development of critical awareness in the students themselves, seen as a target.

The training model used, and the time-scale involved, are outlined in Table 2.

The significant aspects of the strategy were the use of a staged approach and the use of a power-based model as a method of initiating change. Unlike the SCDC/EOC Genderwatch Project (1987) which concentrated on the production of checklists for teachers and the appointment of teachers specifically responsible for equal opportunities in schools, the TREO approach was a top-down one going straight to the sources of power in senior management. The production by headteachers of action plans related to reducing gender inequalities was a key part of the strategy.

The more specific strategies for the various conferences and work-shops were initiated by the two project officers, the two advisers referred to earlier, and outside consultants. These consultants included an Inspector for Equal Opportunities from the Brent LEA,

Table 2 Across school and LEA training model

Tameside	Rochdale
Pre-workshop task of information seeking for headteachers	
Headteacher conferences for all schools, July/September 1986	
Headteachers discuss action plans with deputies	
Deputy headteacher conference for all schools, October 1986	
Middle managers' workshop All schools, Nov. 1986–Feb. 1987	Curriculum working groups Some schools, Oct. 1986–Feb. 1987
Curriculum working group representatives	Middle manager representatives
Project officer support, visits, INSET, July 1986–Aug. 1987	

MSC consultants and a Manchester Polytechnic lecturer involved in the GIST project. Through visits links were made with equal opportunities work in the School Curriculum Development Committee, the ILEA, Birmingham and Manchester. The advice the consultants gave, and the experience gained from the visits, contributed significantly to the project officers' effectiveness.

Throughout the project, connections were made between race and gender, and both the headteachers' and deputy headteachers' conferences included specific sessions on race. It was interesting that at both of these conferences these sessions provoked extreme reactions, either hostile or supportive. This was probably because both sessions sought to deal directly with attitudes in contrast to the sessions on gender which touched upon attitudes but concentrated mainly upon structural change and actions. Reactions were also affected by the make-up of the participants at both conferences. Women were in a minority at both, particularly at the headteachers' conference, but they nevertheless had a presence. While some of the participants felt that it was impossible to draw up action plans for gender without considering race, the majority felt that it was difficult enough coming to terms with gender without complicating the issue with discussions on race. Comments ranged from 'very frustrating, becoming political' to 'thought-provoking – raised issues previously not thought of'. While the institutional nature of sexism has been readily acknowledged, the institutional nature of racism has often been denied. Indeed the use of the word racism has provoked in many a more negative response than the use of the word sexism.

Project INSET

With slight modifications the same programme was used for both of the headteachers' conferences (one a local day conference and the other residential). The course tutor, an Inspector for Equal Opportunities from the Brent LEA, introduced and led sessions for groups on definitions of, and justifications for, equal opportunities, on stereotyping and the hidden curriculum, and on starting points for change. Three headteachers from other LEAs spoke about implementing change in their schools, and the female Deputy Director of Education in the Leicestershire LEA indicated how a LEA policy on equal opportunities could be translated into practice. The final session led to the production of individual action plans after shared brainstorming in small groups.

The conference for the deputy headteachers, organized and led by the two project officers and an MSC consultant, began with an opinion-finding session and groupwork. It continued with active listening and various role-play group exercises, as well as a session on gender and race led by the Rochdale Project Officer. On the final day, a TVEI Regional Adviser led a session on staff development strategies and general management strategies were discussed in groups. The conference ended with the deputies discussing the action plans produced by the headteachers.

The third phase of the project for Tameside provided training for middle managers. A teacher with responsibility for initial course choice and careers work from each college attended a 4-day course. The pre-workshop task was to talk to the deputy and to collect together and bring with them to the course all materials and communications used with pupils and parents relating to options choices. Seven representatives from Rochdale also attended the course. The final day, several months later, was for both the trained middle manager and deputy from each school and focused on the implementation of strategies and sharing experience.

The third phase of the project for Rochdale involved the formation of nine curriculum working groups consisting of 53 teachers (9 from Tameside). Some of these teachers were deputies, some middle managers and many were scale 1 teachers. Each group met separately once a month over 5 months before coming together for a final plenary session. After initial awareness raising sessions they were asked to produce something for use in schools. In the main, working groups concentrated on raising staff awareness through whole-school policies, as they felt this was the most appropriate strategy for change. They produced booklets offering checklists as well as making recommendations; these have been sent to all middle and secondary schools for use in school-based INSET.

The project's impact on schools

The two case studies described below provide examples of how the strategy described operated at the individual school level.

Mixed comprehensive school

In this community school for 11- to 18-year-olds in the Rochdale LEA, five other members of staff were involved in the TREO project as well as the headteacher and one of the deputy headteachers. At the headteachers' conference the following action plan was produced:

- inform and share consultancy with senior management and middle management;
- survey the pupils;
- devise an overall consistent strategy; and
- provide pupils with visible evidence of equality.

After the headteachers' and deputies' conferences a meeting was held for heads of department and heads of year at which there was a presentation of statistics to demonstrate the extent to which there was a 'problem'. In the following term an equal opportunities working party was set up, representative in terms of men and women, junior and senior staff. The main actions taken within the school are as follows:

1 The options booklet has been rewritten as has the first year hand-book to parents.
2 The working party has written an equal opportunities policy statement for the school which was accepted by senior management and submitted to the governing body for approval.
3 From September 1987, all registers and other pupil lists were put in alphabetical order.

4 The working party has turned its attention to information gathering and analysis with a view to a wider dissemination of information to all staff. This has involved the production of a questionnaire for pupils which will help to determine pupil attitudes and perceptions of school policy on the issue of equality.

5 INSET packs have been prepared for subject teachers and for first-year form tutors.

Sixth form college

The first move towards introducing an equal opportunities programme into a sixth form college in Tameside came at the end of the summer term 1986, when a half-day inservice meeting was organized for the staff as an awareness-raising exercise.

Representatives from the college then attended the conferences for headteachers, deputy headteachers, and middle managers. As a result three main aims or action points were decided on for this college:

- the development of an Equal Opportunities Working Party;
- the investigation of 'user friendly' areas in college; and
- the establishment of positive role models.

In response to this plan the main developments within the college were:

1 During the autumn term there was a positive move to establish role models in areas where fewer girls than boys show interest by the giving of responsibility to women members of staff for the development of Information Technology.

2 The Computer Studies Department has improved the environment of its rooms making them more attractive and 'user friendly' and encouraging girls and women to enter the field of computers by organizing two Computer Days for Women as part of Tameside's 'Women's Fortnight'.

3 In the spring term 1987, a working party was set up consisting of those staff who were interested in examining gender issues, looking at the aims and action points with a view to making improvements in the college. The group met weekly and investigated the gender structure of the college, student choices of subject areas and the most effective ways of raising awareness of equal opportunities issues by students and staff (e.g. through the introduction

of an Equal Opportunities module in the General Studies programme and through further INSET for staff).

These two case studies give some indication of the ways in which schools and colleges worked upon the action plans produced by headteachers. These action plans varied from the cosmetic to the radical, but it has been recognized that everyone has to start somewhere and there were very different starting points for individual schools. Some schools have concentrated on organizational matters such as registers and uniform, whereas others went for a whole-school approach together with tackling the hidden curriculum through awareness raising sessions for staff and discussions with governors. Many schools have run their own INSET sessions. The working party approach has proved popular and has served a number of functions including mobilizing concern and marginalizing resistance.

General conclusions

Drawing conclusions about the effect of a project whose life-span was little more than a year is not an easy task. One approach is to take these original criteria for evaluation of the project as set by the management group:

1 Training courses which cover the major arguments in favour of an equal opportunities policy will have been planned and delivered for LEA professional staff, headteachers, deputy head-teachers and teachers in middle and secondary schools.
2 Action plans will have been drawn up in every targeted establishment; project officers will have given support to facilitate development work towards stated goals.
3 Action related to option choice and curriculum development work will have been initiated.
4 The project will have been planned, co-ordinated and delivered by cooperation across the two authorities; staff in both Tameside and Rochdale will have worked together at officer/adviser, head-teacher and teacher levels on equal opportunities initiatives.
5 Contact will have been made with other major LEA and research initiatives on equal opportunities and gender.
6 A base will have been created from which it would be possible to establish specific structures within the two authorities for the

monitoring of progress from the 1986–7 TREO initiative and for future development work.

By these criteria the project may be deemed to be broadly success-ful. But there are further important evaluation questions which remain to be answered. For instance, whether the changes made are only cosmetic can only be judged over a much longer time-scale. In the future any evaluation must include the views of teachers in all schools, the governors, parents, and the students themselves. The middle managers, at their workshop, put high on a list of strategies the need for students to develop skills to be able to recognize and challenge gender stereotyping.

For the present, however, any evaluation of the project can only be based upon the views of the project officers together with those of the external evaluator. The latter commented upon both the TREO training carried out between June 1986 and March 1987 and at the way TREO had developed once transplanted into schools. The observations on the TREO training were as follows:

> Conferences for headteachers and deputy headteachers were designed to draw on a pre-existing bank of commitment towards gender issues among senior managers. The aim was to provide a supportive environment within which heads and deputies could both develop their knowledge of issues around gender equality through formal presentations and explore, through workshops and exercises, the problems they would encounter in practice. For a great many people gender issues were already regarded as an important professional issue before TREO began, but the courses allowed them to translate this concern into action. The role of TREO was to allow time to focus concerns about gender, to provide ideas about how problems could be overcome by breaking them down into a set of manageable actions and to set gender issues firmly on the professional agenda. These aims were broadly achieved.
>
> (North-West TRIST, 1987)

The overall conclusion reached by the external evaluation indi-cates both the achievements of the project and the need for further development work:

> As a strategy for change TREO has been highly successful. It has provided overt and clear support from the LEAs for work on gender – a direct message that such work is a key professional issue.
>
> As a result, during the course of the year, many schools have registered a commitment to change. At an individual level for the

already committed, it has endorsed the work they are doing. For those who were aware of the issues, but were not convinced of the value of the work, or who were perhaps concerned that gender issues might prove difficult and divisive, it has provided practical pointers to change. For the sceptical and unconvinced it has acted as a necessary abrasive. In a few schools, very little movement has taken place for various reasons, but even here there is now a commitment to change. The work that has been initiated in schools is going forward slowly, too slowly for some people who want to see immediate results. But schools are gradually gaining unique insights into the roots of the problems of gender inequality in their schools and work must necessarily proceed with caution.

Firm foundations have been laid for work on gender inequality in Tameside and Rochdale. the LEAs' task for the future is to decide how best to build on and consolidate the work that has been done.

(North-West TRIST, 1987)

In reflecting upon experience of working within the project, as project officers we identified several factors, as discussed below, which were significant in this development process.

Attitude of the headteacher and management style of the school

The headteacher role is ultimately crucial if real change is to take place, but the success of TREO as a strategy for change is that it has tackled schools at different levels, linking training courses together in an attempt to build a team within each establishment.

In some schools, a commitment to equal opportunities has long been shown by many classroom teachers, and many of these became involved in the TREO curriculum working groups. But what was required was to give the ideas and commitment of those teachers a status and a platform. In some schools, a strong committed headteacher was attempting to direct change from the top, but such a headteacher easily became isolated unless the senior management team were supportive. Similarly, some headteachers were not particularly intent on 'delivering' equal opportunities and, in these cases, the role of the senior management team and the initiative of the trained deputy was crucial.

It has become clear that substantial and radical developments to reduce gender inequalities cannot be achieved without a whole-school approach. This does not mean that everyone changes automatically overnight, but rather that a well-organized and systematic approach is taken, with long-term goals in mind achieved through planned stages of development. Those who have tried to compartmentalize work on gender will fail as gender equality must become, in the long term, an integral part of everything a school does, and this will only happen through shorter-term objectives which are closely supported and monitored by a management team with a whole school approach.

Management style is a significant factor in this process; a whole-school approach requires maximum staff awareness and support. Open discussion, debate and consultation produces greater understanding of issues and ownership of developments. In schools with an open consultative style of management, it has been easier for the teachers to accept ideas to reduce gender inequalities as their own and so become committed to change.

The role of the project officers within the LEAs

The project officers brought to the project a variety of experience based on different backgrounds. The Tameside Project Officer was seconded from a position as vice-principal of one of the borough's two sixth form colleges, and had been involved in TVEI work on gender. The Rochdale Project Officer was seconded from his post as acting deputy head at a mixed comprehensive upper school, and was known in the LEA for his work on integrated humanities and multi-cultural/anti-racist education.

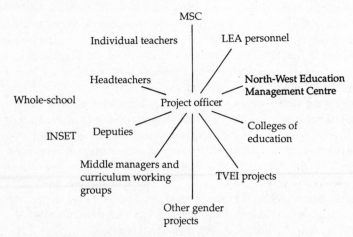

Fig. 1.   The role of project officers within the LEAs.

One important aspect of the project officers' roles was the range of links established with a variety of groups as summarized in Fig. 1.

The existence of project officers as co-ordinators of a specific project rendered headteachers accountable. Each headteacher was asked to indicate how far s/he had progressed with the action plan drawn up at the headteachers' conference. S/he was asked to do this either in a follow-up visit and/or by letter with a follow-up telephone call. It is clear that these acted as reminders and spurs to further developments, helping to keep gender firmly on the agenda for the school.

Working together, rather than in isolation, was a source of strength and the role model of having a man and a woman working together on gender equality proved very effective. It was frequently pointed out that gender stereotyping is as much a straitjacket for boys and men as it is for girls and women.

Our initial work was given a firm and powerful context from the LEAs by the initial letters sent to headteachers from the Chief Education Officers. These letters made it clear that attendance at the conference was expected and that full support should be given. This overt backing gave impact to the project and status to the project officers. The expectation placed upon senior management in schools to make clear progress in terms of gender equality as a mainstream educational issue was a powerful factor in terms of any success the project achieved. We were also able to work through and with advisers in subject areas, with probationary teachers and with support services. The involvement of senior education officers in the management group, fed a constant stream of information by ourselves, maintained a high profile for the project.

The role of the MSC

It could be said of the MSC with some justification that 'the *man* who pays the piper calls the tune'. In recent years, LEA officers have been required to meet specified criteria to obtain much needed funds for innovation in schools: they are then held accountable in relation to those specified criteria for 'delivery'. The Tameside and Rochdale Equal Opportunities pilot project is one example of two LEAs making a successful submission for funds related to their own criteria, based on identified needs and receiving strong backing from the MSC in terms of finance, advice and support.

When the initial approach for funding was made the North-West

TRIST adviser, who was also a member of the MSC National Sub-committee for Equal Opportunities, was quick to make a personal response. From that time, throughout the project, encouragement was given through attendance at management meetings and through involvement in the preparation of the phase 4 dissemination bid, preparation of a TREO booklet for dissemination to every LEA in the country and preparation of an unsuccessful bid for a 2-year extension of the project. In addition, an MSC consultant partici-pated in, and assisted in, the planning of the deputies' conference.

The motives for MSC's stated commitment to equal opportunities in all its aspects have been questioned openly by colleagues, but the fact remains it is a stated commitment. Criteria for YTS, TVEI and TVEI Extension, which include equal opportunities, do two things: they put gender equality higher up the list of priorities than would have been the case otherwise for some colleagues and they give value and status to the work done by many colleagues for years. It is heart-ening to see stated commitment to the issue from a national body with power and money at its disposal.

TVEI criteria for evaluation specifically state that attempts must be made to give equal access to all, and those schools already involved in TVEI were the most receptive to attempts to reduce gender inequalities. As the external evaluation report observes:

> Certain styles of management, in particular an open approach, a dele-gation of issues and a forum for debate through a working party have proved helpful. TVEI schools had often already developed imagin-ative individual approaches to gender issues as a result of the MSC's insistence on equal opportunities. Such schools found TREO extremely helpful in terms of further development. Schools under-taking curriculum reviews or other forms of reorganisation were also 'open' to issues of gender and found the TREO input helpful.
>
> (North-West TRIST, 1987)

As well as the ongoing support and advice given from MSC personnel, the financial backing was of crucial importance. The total sum of £100 000 covered the salaries, expenses and on-costs of the two project officers, finance for supply cover, clerical support, materials and evaluation. The financial backing meant that the materials produced for the conferences and workshops, as well as the booklets produced by the curriculum working groups, were of a reasonable standard of presentation, and were therefore more readily acceptable. Headed notepaper and a specific logo helped add to the professional ethos of the project. Financial support on this scale is important in giving status to a project's activities.

The future

What the TREO project has done is to put equal opportunities firmly on the agenda in both LEAs by raising the awareness of the uncommitted at both the personal and professional levels, and to give status to the ideas and demands of the already committed. A base has been created from which it is possible to establish specific structures for future development work and we have identified for the two LEAs the areas for further development.

- Monitoring and aftercare support for teaching staff.
- Further INSET opportunities.
- Dissemination of the work of curriculum working groups.
- Dissemination to the nursery and primary sector.
- Staffing and recruitment issues.
- Links with the Careers Service.
- Dissemination to parents and governors.
- Development of students' resources.
- Support for action-research.
- Links with cross-curricular multicultural/anti-racist initiatives.

The challenge now for Tameside and Rochdale is to maintain the momentum built up during the induction and dissemination phases of the TREO project, to build upon the foundations established, and through the GRIST programme to establish further action. Like the chocolate biscuit that shares its name, TREO may have been eaten by many in both LEAs, gulped down by some and spat out by others. But the majority are quietly digesting it and need some help. At the time of writing, the secondment of the Rochdale Project Officer has been extended for a year. In Tameside, money was provided through the GRIST programme for a pilot project in six schools which has been co-ordinated by a member of the advisory service with the support of an advisory teacher. The numerous requests for advice and assistance from neighbouring authorities may prompt the MSC to consider again a request for an extension phase to disseminate the work of the project to neighbouring authorities, using the expertise acquired in the two LEAs.

CHAPTER 6

Case Study: Gender Developments in Four Initiatives in Coventry*

VAL MILLMAN

The climate *into* which and the channels *through* which gender issues are introduced, maintained and managed are clearly critical to the success or failure of the strategies that are adopted.

Introduction

As we begin to come to terms with the changes brought about by the Education Act, 1988, we are having to evolve and define equal opportunities issues and practices against a backcloth of rapid change, diminished resources and an uncertain future. In Coventry we have looked to the experiences of such authorities as the ILEA and Brent for strategies and materials which would help to inform our own developments. But while gender initiatives in these LEAs were built in the early 1980s on substantial local resourcing, Coventry's equal opportunities programme has only recently developed in the context of a prolonged period of industrial action and severe budgetary constraint. Under these circumstances, those of us who have been committed to moving this area of work forward have had to develop new skills and strategies. When it has seemed unlikely that equal opportunities would present itself as an arena for change in its own right we have had to look for ways of introducing changes through other channels of educational innovation. In this way, the introduction of

---

* The views expressed in this chapter are those of the author and do not necessarily reflect those of the LEA.

equal opportunities issues into the four pilot projects discussed in this book has been of great significance to wider LEA developments.

My personal involvement in and view of these four projects has varied, as has my role within the authority during the 1980s. What follows in this chapter is my own account and analysis of events, drawn from a variety of sources, not least the experiences and insights of those colleagues alongside whom I have worked over this period of time. It is therefore a personal interpretation of events and does not claim to be representative of the views of the Director of Education or the City Council. In attempting to identify the part that externally funded innovatory projects have played in the development of equal opportunities work in Coventry, it will be important for readers to understand a variety of factors. Equal opportunities initiatives in every LEA have been uniquely shaped by local political, economic, social and cultural contexts. Therefore, it is as crucial to identify key contextual factors as it is to understand equality issues if gender initiatives are to be usefully disseminated across projects and LEAs. The climate *into* which and the channels *through* which gender issues are introduced, maintained and managed are clearly critical to the success or failure of the strategies that are adopted.

Therefore, I shall begin with a brief description of Coventry and the development of its education policies. I shall then trace the growth of interest in gender issues throughout the 1980s, commenting in detail on the place of equal opportunities in the Records of Achievement, Lower-Attaining Pupils, TVEI and TRIST Projects. I shall locate these historically as they were introduced into the authority over this period of time and conclude with some reflections on how these projects have informed (and been informed by) equal opportunities developments in the LEA as a whole.

In using the phrase 'equal opportunities' I shall be referring to the promotion of equality between the sexes. Although in the early 1980s 'equal opportunities' in Coventry was seen to incorporate multicultural and gender issues, more recently the phrase has become synonymous with gender equality. This is for two reasons. First, multicultural and anti-racist education are now more clearly defined as such and, secondly, equal opportunities (gender) is a term many people have become familiar with through exposure to EOC publications and the TVEI criterion. This has been an important means of establishing a broad base of support for gender equality. As we move through 1988, and as there is a growing understanding within the LEA of the relationship between different sources of inequality, it is likely that separate strands of work will be brought together under a common framework. Within this framework, what we have previously described as equal opportunities (gender) will undoubtedly take on a new language and momentum of its own.

The Coventry context

Coventry is a compact city of 310,000 people situated in the West Midlands. Having suffered devasting war damage, the city took great pride in its successful post-war reconstruction and economic 'boom'. During the 1950s women and men came to Coventry from all over Britain and from overseas to join an expanding workforce. As a result, Coventry today has a cosmopolitan community, many of whom remember post-war prosperity with a mixture of nostalgia, bitterness and disbelief.

In contrast, over 16 percent of the adult workforce was unemployed in 1987 (30 percent in the inner-city areas) and only one in ten young people moved into paid employment straight from school. Young black people have found it particularly hard to find paid work. Morale is spasmodically lifted by increased car sales figures, new orders for local products and events such as Coventry's F.A. Cup victory in May 1987! The Labour Council has adopted a number of strategies to promote the city's image and wealth creation, but for many Coventry people with 'little prospect of a significant and real improvement in the local job situation in the immediate future' (Coventry City Council, 1987), it is a time of change and insecurity.

Women have always represented a high proportion (over 40 percent) of the workforce in the West Midlands, although clustered in a narrow range of traditionally female, low-paid, low-status jobs, particularly in the service sector. Women's full-time weekly earnings have consistently been at about 65 per cent of those of men since the Equal Pay Act of 1976! Although the collapse of male-dominated manufacturing industries in recent years has mainly hit male employees, increasing automation has also created redundancies among women in unskilled jobs. The increased availability of part-time employment in the service sector has attracted many women despite unsocial hours and lack of employment protection rights. As many male breadwinners have been made redundant so families have had to adapt to changed working and leisure patterns and new domestic roles. The challenge to Coventry's education service has been to find ways of assisting people in responding positively to such changes.

Education policies

Coventry's education service has developed a distinctive tenor and style in its post-war years. It has responded energetically to new national initiatives and it was one of the first LEAs to adopt the principles of comprehensive education. It has been equally determined to generate its own responses to local needs and has continued to extend its community education policy through primary and secondary schools over the past 15 years. Coventry currently has 19 comprehensives, 116 primary schools, 12 special schools and 4 further education colleges. It has a flourishing teachers' centre which is easily accessible to teachers from all the city's schools.

The accelerated decline of the local economy and changing job market in the mid-1970s marked the beginning of a far-reaching review process of the educational needs of 14- to 19-year-olds. This led to the adoption in 1982 of a series of policy principles and recommendations detailed in a document entitled *Comprehensive Education for Life* (Coventry City Council, 1982). Practical recommendations included the extended development of community colleges, further education provision and modular courses for students from age 14 upwards. The document stressed the importance of 'education for all' and 'education as a life-long process' and it acknowledged the implications of changing trends in local cultures and values. But it carried no explicit reference to the promotion of equality of opportunity. It was considered that the needs of 'disadvantaged' groups were already embraced by a commitment to 'education for all' and that sources of inequality were therefore being tackled. The Minority Group Support Service, for example, had been set up in 1977 to meet the needs of children from New Commonwealth countries and address the implications of their presence in the city. But it was not until 1987 that an education department working party was established to draw up a draft policy and action programme relating to 'race issues'.

Awareness of gender issues in the early 1980s

At national level the early 1980s heralded an accelerating awareness of gender inequality in the field of education. DES and HMI reports were highlighting particular aspects of curricular inequality and

EOC publications were pointing to the 'hidden' as well as to the 'formal' curriculum. Short-term projects such as the Schools Council Sex Differentiation Project (Millman and Weiner, 1985) and the Girls into Science and Technology Project (Kelly *et al.*, 1984) were identifying ways in which teachers could try to challenge these inequalities in their work in schools. At this time in Coventry active consideration of gender issues was restricted to those teachers at a local secondary school where the EOC had recently conducted an investigation into alleged sex discrimination (EOC, 1983), to members of the NUT equal opportunities subcommittee who produced an influential report called *Primary Teachers in Coventry* (NUT, 1984), and to individual teachers in primary and secondary schools who were beginning to meet together to share ideas about curriculum development in this area. In early 1983, after a series of five meetings, a number of secondary teachers produced a report called *Towards Equal Opportunities in Secondary Schools: What Does It Means for Girls?* (Coventry City Council, 1983) and established a permanent equal opportunities curriculum group at the teachers' centre. The group met regularly to organize awareness-raising meetings for secondary teachers working in a variety of subject areas. Later in the year, a member of this group was appointed to the new team of teachers responsible for managing the Lower-Attaining Pupils Programme (LAPP). It was agreed that she should take responsibility within the team for the promotion of equal opportunities (gender). This was the first formal recognition within the LEA of this area of expertise and it is no coincidence that LAPP stands out among Coventry's educational initiatives at this time in its identification of, and discussions around, gender equality.

1983: From small beginnings

Work on Records of Achievement (through the Oxford Certificate of Educational Achievement (OCEA)) and the Lower-Attaining Pupils Programme (named the DES Special Project in Coventry) both began in 1983 when active promotion of equal opportunities in the LEA was still restricted to small committed groups of classroom teachers. The Oxford Certificate of Educational Achievement was one of the nine pilot schemes supported by the government to help develop Records of Achievement by the end of this decade. It has been jointly developed by the University of Oxford Delegacy of Local Examinations, the education authorities of Coventry, Leicestershire, Oxford-shire and Somerset and the University of Oxford Department of Educational Studies. The DES Special Project has provided Coventry, alongside 12 other LEAs, with the opportunity to pilot a curriculum strategy for lower-attaining students which centres around the expanded provision of opportunities for experiential learning. Both projects were shaped and informed by work that had previously taken place within the authority. This had not included any formal discussions of gender issues nor did these feature explicitly in project aims at either local or national level. Despite the differences in the numbers of schools involved, in the ways in which students were selected and in the focus of the new approaches being piloted, both the OCEA and DES Special Projects did offer teachers similar opportunities to bring about change in traditional areas of the curriculum. In both cases teachers were seconded from schools to explore new approaches alongside other teachers, and for those who were aware of gender issues this presented a new forum in which they could ask questions about equal opportunities. However, this largely remained a forum within which the onus rested with the individual teacher. Successful identification of gender issues, there-fore depended as much on the teacher's own level of awareness, confidence, experience and sources of support, as it did on the parti-cular focus of the project to which they were seconded. In the OCEA Project, not only were there few teachers in key positions with exper-ience of identifying gender issues, but those that were aware were not able to bring issues to the forefront of the agenda in the ways that will be described in the DES Special Project.

Oxford Certificate of Educational Achievement

OCEA is essentially a framework for recognizing and recording students' achievements in the widest sense. The student record is compiled over a period of time and has three interdependent com-ponents: a student statement based upon regular reviewing and recording, a statement of curricular achievements and a statement of externally recognized qualifications. Preparatory research and development in each of these components was carried out by seconded teachers at the Delegacy. Their work was 'steered' by com-mittees composed of representatives from the main parties and on a day-to-day basis they consulted reference groups of teachers within each LEA. During the pilot phase of the project, which ran from

September 1985 until March 1988, materials and approaches were trialled in pilot schools.

It was at this time that individual teachers attempted to explore equal opportunities questions and find ways of putting a positive value on the whole range of students' skills and interests, female and male. Some English teachers, for example, found that 'ways of grouping' and 'talking and listening in groups' were fruitful activities through which to explore gender-differentiated aspects of girls' and boys' interaction patterns. But although seconded teachers had successfully pressed for the centrally produced teachers' guides to be multicultural and non-sexist, these materials on their own proved insufficient to generate a challenge to gender differentiation in the classroom of the unaware teacher. In the early days of OCEA, Coventry had no formal mechanisms through which equal opportunities issues and examples of good practice could easily be disseminated either within or between schools. Awareness of gender differences did not therefore spread in any coherent way and individual attempts to pursue positive strategies were not recognized formally in the wider project context.

DES Special Project.

The DES Special Project in Coventry had been set up, like OCEA, without prior consideration of equal opportunities (gender). But two distinctive features of this project's organization led to gender differences becoming much more visible than they had been in OCEA:

1 The secondment to the teacher team of a teacher with substantial experience of promoting equal opportunities.
2 Demonstrable differences between girls and boys in their take-up of the occupational experience component of the special programme.

Having obtained agreement that she should take special responsibility for equal opportunities in the team, the project teacher was well placed to use the evidence of inequality to stimulate positive action.

The new curriculum for the 800 fourth and fifth year students who participated in the project included a day-a-week of 'occupational experience' at a centre designated for education and training programmes. They followed a total of eight 10-week courses at the centre over the 2-year period. Each of the 30 participating schools (comprehensive and special) designated a liaison teacher to plan and review each student's 1-day occupational experience and build links with the student's 4-day school-based curriculum. The Centre Team consisted of eight experienced secondary teachers and 30 skilled supervisors from a variety of craft, commercial and industrial backgrounds. Gender differentiation was apparent from the outset in both the staffing of the project, student selection and take-up of occupational courses at the centre. The predominantly male ethos of the project at staff level was exactly matched at student level with twice as many male as female 'lower attaining' students identified by schools. The centre's programme relied heavily on skilled supervisors who themselves were recruited from Coventry's highly sex-differentiated labour market. Many of these supervisors were able to build strong relationships with students with whom they shared common interests and experiences. These relationships lay at the heart of the project's success but at the cost of an ethos in which it proved very difficult to challenge sex-stereotyped attitudes and behaviour. The division of responsibility among staff and the division of course uptake among students fell into traditionally sex-stereotyped patterns as indicated in Fig. 2.

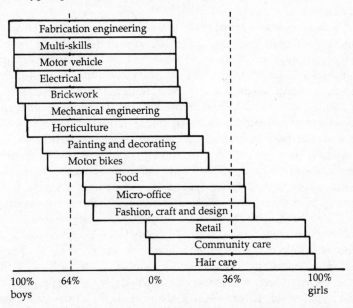

Fig. 2.　Initial LAPP placements of girls and boys in 1983. The long vertical dotted lines represent the overall proportions of girls and boys on this year of the project. (From Coventry City Council, 1984b.)

Given that these sorts of contradictions had not been recognized in the original conception of the project, it rested with the minority of 'aware' teachers to continually register evidence of inequality and gender differentiation and to point to the need for action. Early in the second year of the project, the project teacher with responsibility for equal opportunities circulated an equal opportunities report to the large numbers of personnel involved in the project at LEA, school and centre level. She hoped that a compilation of evidence collected during the first year and a presentation of possible strategies would spread awareness and stimulate action, although clearly this would have to be backed up by inservice training if any coherent project strategies were to emerge. In discussion with the centre teacher team a number of problem areas were identified which needed to be tackled. Some of these, such as student selection, lay in the hands of the schools; others, such as the shortage of 'neutral' and traditionally female areas on offer to students, had deep-seated implications for the purchasing of new equipment and the appointment of new supervisors. Some needed to be tackled directly with the supervisors, e.g. the sexual harassment of girls in the work areas or the domination of boys in mixed groups.

The teacher team agreed that it should start by tackling the areas most immediately under its control. This included the role models the project teachers themselves presented and the measures they could take to promote equality in their day-to-day contacts with supervisors and liaison teachers and in the administrative tasks they undertook. They could, for example, ensure that individual girls and boys were not isolated in non-traditional occupational areas. Next they would raise the issues with liaison teachers at their weekly meetings, involve them in a programme of observation of student interaction in the occupational areas and suggest that they take their findings back to discuss with colleagues and students at school. This programme proved a successful means of awareness-raising at centre level, although, with the yearly changeover of liaison teachers, it is doubtful whether any sustained change was achieved back in schools. The centre teacher team agreed to postpone equal opportunities inservice training with supervisors until later. Although the supervisors' influence on the sex-stereotyped ethos of the project was clearly powerful, it was felt that their resistance to the issues and their understandable preoccupation with acquiring new instructional skills and solving practical problems in their work areas would have made them unreceptive to INSET at this stage. It was considered that ill-timed INSET might have closed off opportunities for raising the issues at a future date.

During the first 2 years of the DES Special Project it was difficult for those who had been trying to increase awareness of the problem to see visible signs of success. They still felt relatively isolated and unable to bring about significant practical changes at either centre or school level. Their position was not strengthened by the fact that neither HMI nor members of the NFER evaluation team on their visits to the project had identified the evidence of gender differences as an issue. These teachers felt that they had achieved little change within the project with the occupational experience component remaining male-dominated and sex-stereotyped at staff and student level, and little understanding gained about the relationship between gender and low attainment.

Perhaps they had set their sights too high. They had been appointed to a project which had been speedily set up without prior discussion of equal opportunities in relation to staff and student selection criteria. The project structures were, therefore, sex-stereotyped from the outset and there remained little time in which to bring about change. Seeking support from colleagues and increasing awareness from the centre outwards were in fact significant components of a long-term change process which would undoubtedly have been brought forward if there had been more support for equal opportunities work within and beyond the project. These teachers had capitalized on the unprecedented forum offered by the DES Special Project for discussions among teachers across all Coventry's comprehensive and special schools, and had succeeded in significantly heightening the awareness of the issues at secondary level within the LEA. When TVEI came to the authority during the second year of the DES Project, some of the most difficult groundwork of awareness-raising had already taken place.

1984–5: Moving up the agenda

When Coventry launched its TVEI Project in September 1984, it had few coherently formulated strategies to draw upon in trying to meet the MSC's equal opportunities criterion. Student take-up in the first cohort revealed 39 per cent of girls as compared with 61 per cent of boys across the three project schools. This pattern was similar for the second cohort the following year. The TVEI central team recognized that a more coherent whole-school approach would be needed to counteract the sex-stereotyping indicated by these patterns and, in the Autumn of 1985, a Teacher Adviser for Equal Opportunities (Gender) was appointed to work with the pilot schools. During this period the LEA had also been engaged in a consultation process about responses to falling rolls in Coventry's schools. Draft proposals for the future organization of schools were put forward in *Future Choices: Meeting the Challenges* (Coventry City Council, 1985). This document contained Coventry's first public statement of commitment to the 'equality of status, opportunities and dignity of women with men', and proposed:

> that single sex secondary schools should gradually develop as co-educational schools. This should be seen in the light of our proposal for the development of equal opportunities within schools. (p. 7)

> . . . a programme of review and development to be promoted and sustained to ensure equal opportunities throughout the school system. (p. 6)

At this time, equal opportunities was seen to incorporate multi-cultural and gender issues. The immediate outcome of the consultation process was that three schools went co-educational, two through amalgamation. The debates around single-sex/co-educational schooling had considerably heightened teacher and public awareness of gender issues in education and the transition of three schools to co-education provided an important stimulus for the provision of teacher INSET in equal opportunities. Teachers at other secondary schools who had been among the first to recognize the problem of sex differentiation some years earlier, were now becoming less isolated and increasingly recognized as an important source of expertise in this area. Some of these teachers were based in TVEI schools and were able to play a significant part in shaping whole-school approaches.

Technical and Vocational Educational Initiative

THE FIRST TWO YEARS
At the outset the LEA established a central team with a project co-ordinator to administer and manage the pilot project. Additional staffing was also allocated to each of the four participating institutions (three schools and one further education college) to support a

project co-ordinator and technical and teaching staff. At the heart of the Coventry scheme is a modular course. Students have the opportunity to complete 14 TVEI modules over 2 years in addition to an 'inner core' of subjects and options. Student take-up of options and modules showed evidence of sex-stereotyping from the outset.

Although there was general sympathy towards equal opportunities from the beginning of the project, especially among members of the central team, action during the first year was generally restricted to one-off initiatives such as theatre workshops and 'persuasive counselling' at option choice time; staff were also released to attend MSC equal opportunities conferences. School management was understandably preoccupied with making new appointments, bringing in new equipment and setting up new courses. Although cross-curricular themes are prioritized in the Coventry scheme, continuous pressure had to be exerted on pilot institutions by the central co-ordinator to 'give active support to equal opportunities by setting up teams' in schools. It was felt that the appointment of the teacher adviser referred to earlier would be an important means of sustaining this pressure and developing informed whole-school approaches during the second year of the project.

This appointment coincided with an intensified period of industrial action by teachers so that the teacher adviser's consistent argument for equal opportunities to be built into the schools' mainstream structures rather than rely on 'goodwill meetings' carried an increased sense of urgency. Without designated responsibility and non-contact time for meeting and development work there was little prospect of changed practice. The case for this level of investment of resources by schools had to be thoroughly debated at TVEI headteachers and co-ordinators meetings and the TVEI Residential Conference in January 1986. For many, this involved extending their previously narrow definitions of equal opportunities – such as getting more girls into CDT – to an acknowledgement of the need for a long-term, whole-school strategy that tackled not only the formal TVEI curriculum but also the 'hidden curriculum' of the school. This hidden curriculum included an examination of staffing structures and questioned the effect on students of TVEI appointments made in the first year – 3 of the new appointments and promotions had been women compared with 17 men! Although this shift in definition of the problem appeared to be accepted, there were pressures to adopt quick, simple, high-profile strategies.

TVEI's contractual requirement to LEAs to meet its equal opportunities criterion in a short period of time perhaps made this pressure inevitable. Added to this was the fact that it was mainly men with little knowledge of equal opportunities work who were expected to manage the response to this pressure. The nature of the goals set, and the ways in which they aimed to achieve them, therefore, tended to be substantially at odds with much of the developmental work pioneered by some LEAs earlier in the 1980s (Millman and Weiner, 1987). The teacher adviser argued that for short-term, high-profile initiatives to be helpful to students it was necessary to secure them in the context of a whole-school strategy. To achieve this it was necessary to argue for the recognition of equal opportunities as an area of expertise based on experience and knowledge of the issue which needed to be identified, supported and developed within each institution. It was not a common-sense issue that could be taken on board by any old Tom, Dick or Harry!

TVEI ENTERS ITS THIRD YEAR: MORE CONCERTED ACTION
In the Autumn of 1986, the TVEI Project entered its third year. Some changes had already been initiated by the central team in an attempt to offer a more balanced course to students. New modules were made available to the third cohort of students which aimed to recognize traditionally female skills and interests. The evaluator commented that 'the new modules . . . did indeed offer a more creative and aesthetic dimension as well as more vocationally biased modules such as food technology' (Batts, *et al.*, 1985). Two schools significantly increased their uptake by girls in the third cohort so that the overall composition was now 44 per cent girls and 56 per cent boys. By the fourth year of the project nearly all fourth and fifth year students in two of the three pilot schools were on TVEI courses; this ensured a female:male take-up proportional to the balance of the school population.

In schools, there were significant moves towards identifying equal opportunities goals and setting up appropriate structures. Each school identified a senior member of staff to take responsibility for oversight of equal opportunities developments. Each school also released a member of staff for one morning a week for meetings of the new TVEI Equal Opportunities Curriculum Group. These three teachers met weekly with the teacher adviser throughout the third year of the project. The aims of the group meetings were to provide support and inservice training for group members as well as to work with other TVEI curriculum groups to stimulate awareness and positive action in specific subject areas. The group felt some conflict at first between satisfying its own need for an exploratory period (to view possible strategies against each school's level of awareness, priorities, etc.) and meeting management's and teachers' expectations that they would come up with a 'product' to solve the 'equal opportunities problem'. Senior staff in schools who were new to equal opportunities issues themselves felt under pressure to 'achieve equal opportunities' and they looked to the curriculum group for the solution. In an attempt to extend senior management's understanding of the processes of change involved, during the project's third year the teacher adviser suggested that a deputy head from each school should attend a national equal opportunities conference at which the 'Genderwatch' (Myers, 1987) materials were launched. Although in the short term this caused some resentment among committed classroom teachers who had not been offered similar opportunities for outside stimulus and access to classroom materials, it did appear to increase an appreciation of the issues at senior level.

At this time a variety of activities were being developed within the pilot schools. A number of administrative changes were made, some more successful than others. In one school a proposal to address all women teachers as 'Ms' in written communications stimulated lively discussion but no change! Another aspect of the hidden curriculum that was examined was staffing structures, in particular the ways in which senior jobs could be redefined and presented in advertisements to encourage applications from women. A number of departments launched their own initiatives, e.g. plays, videos and equal opportunities weeks. Members of the curriculum group helped to support and evaluate these activities and point to new 'action' areas. Their progress was sometimes hindered by a lack of school structures appropriate to the investigation of whole-school issues. For example, when the group decided to investigate a variety of influences which might underlie sex-stereotyped choice at option choice time, teachers discovered that the option and modular data were not readily accessible in schools and there was no annual option choice review process built into the senior management timetable.

The success of many initiatives during the third year, therefore, depended largely on the network of relationships, personal stamina and skills of the initiators. The project evaluator rightly pointed out that a greater formalization and integration of equal opportunities into school structures would put less of a drain on the skills, energy and ingenuity of committed individuals and equal opportunities curriculum group members (Merson 1987). (This principle is as relevant to the effectiveness of equal opportunities working parties as it is to individuals with designated responsibility.) At the beginning of the fourth year, schools allocated additional non-contact time to group members to co-ordinate in-school initiatives, but ready access of these members to school decision-making bodies still varied from school to school.

Many issues emerged during the process of evolving equal opportunities strategies within TVEI that have raised fundamental questions about both innovation and current educational procedures and practices. While equal opportunities developments took a distinctive form in each institution, a number of common points emerged from the work of the curriculum group:

- The need to adopt a whole-school strategy that embraced the experience and energy of already aware and committed teachers.
- The development of approaches that involved key individuals and groups.
- The need to adopt a range of working styles in order to gain acceptance and credibility with a diversity of school staff.

In relation to this latter point, approaches that proved most successful with women teachers – informal discussions which linked personal with professional gender issues – were often a 'turn-off' to male colleagues who felt more comfortable with formal presentations of facts and figures. This generated a particular set of tensions around an issue where most expertise was in the hands of women teachers in junior positions in school and not in the hands of the predominantly male decision-makers.

1986–7: Moving into higher gear within the LEA

As TVEI had entered its third year in 1986 with the introduction of new course modules, the establishment of a central equal opportunities curriculum group and the commitment of pilot schools to the adoption of whole-school approaches, other equal opportunities initiatives were also moving into higher gear within the LEA. The teacher adviser's responsibilities were extended beyond TVEI to promote equal opportunities across the LEA. The three schools that had 'gone co-ed' were continuing their equal opportunities discussions and the LAPP teacher team was planning inservice training for the project supervisors. Most significantly, in December 1986, the LEA set up an Equal Opportunities (Gender) Steering Group. The establishment of the steering group and the appointment shortly afterwards of a new Chief Education Officer publicly committed to prioritizing equal opportunities policies, both added considerable impetus to existing equal opportunities initiatives. The brief of the steering group was to examine and make recommendations on the promotion of gender equality at the level of both curriculum and staffing through from nursery to higher education. Membership was based on knowledge and experience of gender issues. The steering group provided the first formal forum within the LEA in which those who had pioneered classroom work in the early 1980s could exchange ideas and experiences with those who had moved in more recently through their experience of LAPP, TVEI and the transition of single-sex schools to co-education. The importance of the steering group's discussions and recommendations was signalled by the Director of Education in the following extract from a letter to head-teachers in April 1987:

> The attention the Authority and the service is preparing to give to the problems of inequality and sex stereotyping must be given a definite and authoritative place on our agendas. We have a choice as to whether we respond to the problems at a cosmetic or serious level and the Authority's intention is to treat them seriously.

It was during this period, in the year prior to the establishment of its GRIST (Grant-Related Inservice Training) Programme that the LEA's first equal opportunities INSET courses were being organized for teachers by the teacher adviser. Initially, these aimed to support those teachers who were already working in this area, within TVEI and the DES Special Project for example. Often they were a means of helping these teachers to raise the awareness of their colleagues. It was at this time that the DES Special Project Team approached the teacher adviser to help them organize an INSET programme for the project supervisors whom they now felt were better prepared to take equal opportunities issues on board. The teacher team were reluctant to lead these discussions with supervisors in an apparently 'high-risk' area where they felt unsure of themselves. A programme involving contributions from visiting speakers working in non-traditional roles was therefore worked out and implemented jointly at the teachers' centre. Despite early reservations about the importance or usefulness of the course, the supervisors were visibly 'won over' after the first 40 minutes of the visitors' talks, and they participated in the remaining sessions in a lively, forthright and constructive manner.

Another aspect of the 1986–7 inservice training programme was the opportunity for the teacher adviser to work with seconded teachers who were in key positions to explore equal opportunities issues with teachers in schools. It was at this stage that OCEA secondees recognized the need to explore aspects of OCEA practice in greater depth and discuss issues raised by Sue O'Neill's checklist 'Records of Achievement: Pupil Profiles' in the Genderwatch pack (Myers, 1987). Following this they began working on a set of guidelines for use by OCEA schools and colleges and discussed how equal opportunities might be included in the project's local monitoring procedure.

TVEI-Related Inservice Training

The potentially powerful role of short-term seconded teacher teams in promoting equal opportunities within and across projects is best illustrated by a detailed examination of Coventry's TRIST Team which was established in January 1986. The TRIST team consisted of five professional tutors responsible to a member of the Authority's advisory service. The two female tutors, whose specialist areas were science and information technology, had both had experience of raising gender issues with colleagues and students in their schools. The three male tutors characterized themselves as holding 'open liberal attitudes' and a 'sympathy to the issues'. The tutors were based at the teachers' centre where they spent one day a week participating in their own inservice training programme. In their work in secondary schools they aimed to identify and work with individual departments and classroom teachers who were well-placed to develop and promote the teaching styles and methodologies (e.g. active learning) at the heart of the TRIST team's approach. The project was steered over its four-term period by a Steering Group consisting of LEA officers and advisers, and an MSC representative.

There were two main reasons for the prominence given to gender issues by the TRIST Project. First, the fact that it was 'TVEI-related' and that equal opportunities was becoming increasingly central to TVEI and LEA practice at secondary level and, secondly, the tutors'

2-week induction period and weekly inservice sessions provided time and space for continuous review and development of a number of issues including gender. The adviser responsible for team co-ordination built equal opportunities into the TRIST inservice programme from the start; the Teacher Adviser for Equal Opportunities (Gender) was invited to join the TRIST Steering Group and contribute to inservice training of TRIST tutors. This level of commitment was reinforced by Coventry's participation in the TRIST-sponsored West Midlands Regional Project to promote the professional development of women teachers.

Equal opportunities inservice training of the professional tutor team during the induction period involved the TRIST team adviser, equal opportunities teacher adviser and the five professional tutors. The TRIST team's INSET programme aimed to provide members with regular opportunities to review their progress on equal opportunities individually and collectively over the four-term period of the project. At the end of this period the programme was evaluated in relation to its effect on levels of awareness and working practices within the team, as well as to its translation into changed practice within schools. When interviewed for the evaluation report (Millman, 1987) one tutor commented on the personal tensions that were inevitably generated in inservice training on equal opportunities:

> It had not occurred to me before how important the aspect of 'equal opportunities' being personal as well as professional was. This was rammed home at the INSET session we did for TVEI.

The report reveals that all tutors felt that their own INSET sessions had influenced the operation of the team and interaction of team members as well as their professional practice in schools. Both women tutors felt that equal opportunities had strengthened their position in relation to the potential dominance of male tutors/team leader. Two of the male tutors felt that they had become aware of group dynamics and the need to adjust their behaviour in certain situations. Those who had not previously been actively involved in this area of work all agreed that 'it is far more difficult than I had previously thought'. They all stressed the importance of having a sense of humour to provide a cushion against the levels of resistance that are frequently experienced. They now recognized that it is not possible to bring about *professional* change without personal commitment in this area and it is therefore an extremely sensitive area to tackle. Tutors felt there were parallels with the sort of changes in teaching/learning styles they were trying to bring about through TRIST. They concluded that while all teachers are capable of some change, it is essential to start by working with those who already have a positive level of awareness.

The acceleration of tutors' involvement in promoting gender equality over the course of the four-term project was remarkable and attributable to a number of factors, not least the membership and composition of the team itself. Building an explicit commitment to equal opportunities into team practice from day one short-circuited some of the early problems of the TVEI and DES Special Projects. The strong personal relationships between the team and the teacher adviser for equal opportunities combined with their location in the same building meant easy access to advice and resources. For the teacher adviser too, this meant ready access to a high-status professional team with inroads into most of Coventry's secondary schools as well as other LEA initiatives such as the development of modular courses. Even where the TRIST work was not explicit in its promotion of gender equality, it prepared the ground in crucial ways for challenging traditional styles of classroom organization, changing the whole-school ethos, examining personal and professional practices and adopting new approaches to inservice training.

Despite the TRIST team's successes in promoting equal opportunities in schools and on courses, the extent to which they were able to change practices appeared to be limited by three factors:

1 Even teachers who were highly committed to equal opportunities were reluctant to make changes in classroom organization/curriculum content that might put at risk their class discipline, their image/status in the eyes of students, colleagues, parents, and their ability to complete the course syllabus.

2 A requirement to promote gender equality arrives alongside a requirement to introduce many other changes which involve an increased workload for students and teachers. In such situations it was often the professional tutors' and teachers' judgement to leave equal opportunities 'until later'.

3 A 'lipservice' statement of support for equal opportunities sometimes obstructed the progress of tutors who were only able to discern a lack of real commitment as the period of their 'contract' neared its end.

While the above limitations are apparent in all equal opportunities

development work they are more difficult to overcome in a programme based on short-term interventions from outside the school.
At the end of the four-term period the MSC-funded TRIST Project
became the LEA's Secondary Curriculum Support Team. Three
tutors left the project at the end of their secondment and advertisements for their replacement specifically required candidates to
demonstrate a commitment to equal opportunities. The new team
consisted of four women and one man. The new Secondary Curriculum Support Team adopted a new strategy. Schools were asked to
involve staff with equal opportunities responsibility or expertise in
the initial negotiations of the team's support programme in schools.
In this way it was hoped to stimulate the establishment of links and
structures within the school which would sustain longer-term
development of 'good equal opportunities practice'.

1988: Where are we now and what have we learnt?

The centrality of equal opportunities issues in the TRIST project
helped to establish approaches to inservice training which have
featured prominently in this year's GRIST programme. At the secondary level, equal opportunities courses have formed a significant
part of daytime INSET provision. These courses have recognized the
particular importance of well-organized, well-resourced INSET in
areas where people are likely to be sceptical or hostile and in which
their cooperation is needed in order to bring about changed attitudes
and behaviour. Courses have been designed to meet the needs of the
variety of whole-school approaches which have been developing
over the past couple of years. Although almost all secondary schools
are now taking initiatives in this area of work, a variety of models
has evolved. A number of schools have working parties, some have
posts of responsibility. Others have focused on the issues through a
series of discrete 'equal opportunities' events such as a visit of the
'WISE Bus' or a third-year option choice programme. At individual
school level, as at LEA level, the exploratory groundwork has
preceded the process of policy formulation. This policy-making process has now been formally initiated within the Education Department of the City Council; the recommendations of the LEA Gender
Steering Group have formed the basis of consultations with
interested parties.
 The INSET programme has aimed to support and inform the
development of individual school approaches and help schools to

review and evaluate their progress. It has been specifically targeted at various groups: senior management and equal opportunities post holders, pastoral and departmental teams, members of school working parties as well as groups of classroom teachers. During this year all secondary schools are moving into the TVEI extension phase and the TVEI equal opportunities curriculum group has played a key role in pushing equal opportunities higher up secondary school agendas. The group's work has aimed to help extension schools to learn from the pilot phase that both curriculum and staffing structures must reflect equal opportunities perspectives from the outset if students are to experience equality of opportunity within the TVEI programme. The group has produced a 'strategy' resource pack as a basis for inservice training with all secondary schools. The pack contains guidelines drawn from examples of good practice which it is hoped will form a basis on which schools can build their own models of change.

The GRIST programme and the work of the LEA Gender Steering Group referred to earlier have both provided opportunities during the past year for considerable dissemination of good practice. This has marked the beginning of a process of integration of ideas and approaches which have a variety of origins – the transition to co-education, NUT equal opportunities groups, the short-term externally-funded pilot projects such as LAPP or TVEI. The establishment and part-time staffing of a resource base and the publication of newsletters and course reports have also been significant in generating wider awareness and discussion of the issues. The very process of integration makes the task of identifying critical factors retrospectively a difficult one.

However, the remainder of this chapter will attempt to do this specifically in relation to the four secondary projects discussed in this book. Equal opportunities work that has been explored within these pilot projects has clearly played a significant role in informing wider LEA developments. It is useful to reflect on what we have learnt, particularly in relation to introducing equal opportunities into a context increasingly shaped by external pressure for change.

The significance of the four pilot projects for gender developments

PROJECT STRUCTURE

The pilot nature of all four projects presented opportunities for changed practice within schools; each of them challenged traditional school practices, some across a wider area than others. Those that required an examination of whole-school ethos in addition to a review of curricular practice provided fertile ground for the promotion of equal opportunities. The depth to which gender issues could become firmly embedded on the ground depended on a variety of factors. Each project's aims and objectives were different and these differences informed the strategies that were adopted in order to achieve specific goals. The MSC's emphasis on the 'technical' and 'vocational' nature of TVEI and Coventry's decision to have an occupational experience foundation to its LAPP project led to sex-stereotyped project structures inextricably linked with initiatives of a traditional vocational nature. While the MSC's first contractual requirement to LEAs to 'provide equal opportunities for young people of both sexes' provided a powerful means of prioritizing the 'notion' of gender equality, the technical and vocational emphasis of the project set some limitations on its translation into practice. Although all projects stressed that successful educational outcomes for students are dependent on an emphasis on learning 'processes', the outcomes expected of the projects themselves in a short time-scale shaped the approaches they were able to adopt. In some ways the OCEA and TRIST approaches provided more fertile ground in which to promote gender equality than TVEI and LAPP. The former projects explicitly invited review and re-definition of the hidden curriculum as well as of the formal curriculum. The timing of the introduction of OCEA and TRIST in relation to the development of Coventry's commitment to equal opportunities meant that only a few individual teachers succeeded in taking advantage of the opportunities offered by OCEA; the TRIST team, starting later, was in a stronger position to encourage participating secondary schools to consider gender issues as a priority.

The TRIST Project is a useful illustration of how far the high prioritization of gender issues can result in changed practice within a short-term project and of which factors influence the extent of change. The fact that the TRIST tutors, with little experience of bringing about change in this area, quickly grasped the issues and learned appropriate skills, demonstrates the potential of intensive and continuous inservice training in a context which prioritizes rather than marginalizes the issues. The problem for the tutors was to apply strategies developed in a supportive climate to school contexts which varied in receptiveness and in which many competing demands were being made on both management and classroom teachers. There was a limit to how much change could be instigated in a short period *and* to the nature of the change that could be achieved. Tutors had to be aware that the personal–professional dimension of gender equality made it a sensitive high-risk area of change, difficult to introduce through short-term interventions from outside an institution. The TRIST team had to learn to set realistic goals both for themselves and with the teachers in schools.

REALISTIC GOAL SETTING

Goal setting is as important in equal opportunities work as in any other area of innovation and development. Public goal setting is a powerful means of pressurizing those involved to resource appropriate strategies adequately. TVEI has demonstrated the power of its equal opportunities criterion in propelling pilot projects towards the achievement of 'equal opportunities'. But the MSC's lack of definition, and most LEAs' lack of experience of gender issues, led many projects to set highly inappropriate goals, particularly in the early days. MSC's sophisticated system of data collection and analysis illustrated to LEAs how useful figures can be to illustrate the problem of sex-stereotyping but, in the absence of a broader understanding of underlying gender equality issues and under pressure to act quickly, many project personnel equated equal opportunities with option choice figures and mistakenly searched for 'simple cause and effect' approaches (MSC, 1987a). This definition of equal opportunities appeared to lend itself to straightforward evaluation; unfortunately, it was also doomed to failure without accompanying strategies to tackle the plethora of influences which lead to sex-stereotyped choices.

By the second year of its project, Coventry TVEI had sought to broaden its definitions of equal opportunities and redefine its goals. The appointment of the teacher adviser with experience and knowledge of the latest research and curriculum development on gender issues, combined with the involvement in schools of teachers with equal opportunities expertise, were both crucial to the setting of informed and realistic goals. This expertise has prevented unnecessary 'reinvention of the wheel', while at the same time emphasizing the importance of each school collecting and analysing its own data – including qualitative data – reaching its own diagnosis of problems, needs and possible solutions. The key issues may present themselves very differently in mixed and single-sex schools, for example. Our experience has demonstrated that this process is best begun with key groups of staff which include both those committed to equal opportunities issues and those responsible for the successful management of the project. Subsequently, each school has to make judgements about how best to involve other teaching and non-teaching staff over a period of time, and how fast it can move from awareness raising to policy formulation, changed practice and dissemination of successful strategies. Within each of these areas, goals have to be set and regularly reviewed. It is important that under pressure to 'come up with the goods', schools do not become over-competitive and adopt inappropriate strategies; the teacher adviser's experience and position aimed to help schools develop confidence in making these judgements.

DESIGNATED RESPONSIBILITY FOR EQUAL OPPORTUNITIES
The appointment of individuals with equal opportunities responsibility at LEA advisory level or within schools is often viewed with apprehension; it is felt that *everyone* within the education service should take responsibility for promoting gender equality. In Coventry, experience within TVEI, for example, had indicated that, before this stage could be reached, visible well-defined strategies needed to be adopted that pushed equal opportunities centre-stage. The appointment of a teacher adviser and the allocation of time and responsibility to teachers in schools were two such strategies. The extent of influence of individuals with equal opportunities responsibilities will obviously depend on a range of enabling factors: their location centrally or marginally within LEA/school structures; the extent to which their developmental work is supported by LEA/school policies; the time and money they have available to them. Their own commitment to, and experience of, equal opportunities work, together with the support available to them to continuously challenge colleagues and structures, will obviously also influence their effectiveness. Within these parameters, individuals with designated responsibility can exercise considerable influence. This influence can often be achieved by asking the right questions of the right people at the right time. Given that equal opportunities is a perspective that cuts across every aspect of the education service, rather than a product that can be slotted into one place at one moment in time, it is important to work with key individuals and groups to formulate answers to those questions. Coventry's experience of Records of Achievement, LAPP, TVEI and TRIST indicate that there is a need for informed questions about gender to be asked

at every stage of project submission, formulation, implementation and evaluation. The teacher adviser can apply a checklist of questions to this process:

- How is equal opportunities expressed in the original LEA submission? Is an explicit commitment to gender equality consistent with other aspects of the proposed project and the presentation of the project itself?
- How are schools helped to interpret this equal opportunities commitment in practice? What resources will be allocated to the promotion of equal opportunities in terms of teacher time, materials, INSET provision etc.?
- How can we ensure that new appointments and promotions promote equal opportunities in terms of positive role models for students?
- What structures and mechanisms will be needed to achieve continuous monitoring and review of progress towards equal opportunities within the project?

The fact that an individual has been appointed specifically to ask such questions demands considered responses. The involvement of Coventry's teacher adviser in preliminary TVEI extension consultations with headteachers ensured that gender issues were registered in discussions from the very beginning. Given the increase in central government initiatives to which LEAs and schools are currently being asked to respond, individuals with equal opportunities responsibilities need their own 'think-tanks' to help them interpret and define questions, issues, mechanisms and action – plans which will be central to the context of a new project. In Coventry, the TVEI equal opportunities group provided such a forum for staff from schools; the LEA teacher adviser was also able to have discussions with colleagues in other LEAs. The role of the teacher adviser centrally within the LEA and her membership of key committees has facilitated the development, monitoring and dissemination of equal opportunities initiatives within the TVEI and TRIST Projects. TVEI headteachers' and co-ordinators' meetings require regular progress reports on equal opportunities. A similar mechanism within the DES Special Project in 1984 would have quickly thrown up the disparity between numbers of girls and boys selected for the project and reparative action would have been required. The teacher adviser's membership of the LEA advisory team and other project steering groups has helped to build cross-project links and encouraged a sharing of ideas. Project personnel from TRIST and TVEI, for example, have been brought together to discuss gender issues and devise approaches to inservice training of colleagues. This has helped to promote a coherence of approaches, especially within INSET, which strengthens the identity of equal opportunities curriculum development across the authority. In turn, this has reduced the stress on individuals with equal opportunities responsibility whose work has been given increased legitimacy. It has also recognized the equal opportunities expertise of individual classroom teachers by releasing them for INSET and publishing their materials. In some cases, senior management in schools has felt uneasy about equal opportunities innovation where the major source of expertise often lies in the hands of junior (female) members of staff. At times the teacher adviser has helped restore confidence to both parties and has been able to identify a meaningful context in which they can communicate about complex aspects of gender equality.

Looking forward

In 1988 in Coventry much of our thinking about equal opportunities practices has derived from the experiences of secondary schools, many of which have been involved in at least one of the four government-funded initiatives explored in this book. Equal opportunities issues have been located and expressed differently within each project. This chapter has tried to analyse the differences so that future responses to new initiatives can be thoroughly informed and visibly successful in promoting gender equality. In Coventry, we are now well-placed to extend equal opportunities more widely across the authority and to develop an informed and effective equal opportunities policy within the City's educational institutions. The compactness of the LEA lends itself well to rapid dissemination and integration of new ideas and approaches. The Primary and Further/Higher Education Subcommittees of the LEA Gender Steering Group made a number of recommendations for broadening the focus of equal opportunities developments, and pilot work in these areas is now underway. In the coming years new government initiatives will offer LEAs a series of opportunities and constraints. The challenge to our education service will be to use the growing level of equal opportunities commitment and expertise to ensure that our responses are equally well-matched to the needs of both girls and boys, women and men from all corners of the Coventry community.

Acknowledgements

I would like to thank colleagues, friends and family to whom I have turned for professional comment, secretarial assistance and support during the period of co-editing this book and writing about gender developments in Coventry. I would particularly like to thank all those whose sustained practical commitment to equal opportunities has been responsible for the positive developments referred to in this chapter.

CHAPTER 7

Feminism, Equal Opportunities and Vocationalism: the Changing Context

GABY WEINER

The 1980s has seen sustained growth of interest in gender issues and a strengthening criticism of the continued existence of sex-differentiated education. They have also been years of intense activity by 'radical' conservative administrations bent on bringing schools closer to the world of work. Moreover, one feature of this 'vocationalizing' of education has been the promotion of equal opportunities. The coexistence of these two educational policies has led me to ponder on the implications of the educational changes of the 1980s for feminists. This chapter, then, examines what seems to be the unusual marriage between the 'new vocationalism' and equal opportunities.

That schooling could and should have a stake in the shaping of the workforce is far from new. According to Williams (1961), from the sixth century onwards the first English schools had a primarily vocational intent, that of training priests and monks. In the middle ages education was orientated towards craft apprentices, future knights and aspiring clerics and the eighteenth century saw the growth of new vocational academies serving commerce, engineering and the armed services. It was only at the time of the Industrial Revolution that educationists claimed a distinction between learning for its own sake and for the needs of the state.

Historically, the exclusion of women from public life was paralleled by their exclusion from public schooling. With the advent of a state schooling system in the nineteenth century, debates about

vocational education focused on male rather than female pupils and
workers. The home rather than the factory was seen as the 'natural'
destination of girls and women. Hence the school curriculum firmly
directed girls towards forms of domestic employment, either as
mothers or as servants (Davin, 1979). What is significant about
recent discussions concerning the relationship between schooling
and the wage labour market is the inclusion of examination of gender
differentiation, and its implications.

Despite the 'reconstructionist' ethic of the 1940s, the Labour
administrations of the 1960s and 1970s and the feminist lobbies
arising from the Women's Liberation Movement, the first major
gender initiative in education was created by the Manpower Services
Commission (MSC). The MSC, established in 1973, had become a
powerful government agency principally responsible for the promotion of training for employment (McCulloch, 1987). Prior to the
gender initiative, tentative steps towards providing opportunities
for women had already been made through the Training Opportunities Scheme (TOPS) and Wider Opportunities for Women (WOW).
However, the MSC had found it particularly difficult to redirect
young women in the new youth training programmes (YOP, and
later, YTS) towards 'non-traditional' crafts. This was caused, it was
believed, by young women's lack of school experience in science and
technology.

The next step was to intervene in the development of the secondary school curriculum. In 1984, MSC identified sex-stereotyping as
an obstacle to educational progress and announced that with respect
to the Technical and Vocational Educational Initiative (TVEI), a
criterion for funding would be that:

> equal opportunities should be available to people of both sexes and
> they should normally be educated together on courses within each
> project. Care should be taken to avoid sex-stereotyping. (MSC,
> 1984a)

This statement, then, emerged from a government whose overt
political and economic commitment was towards giving free rein to
the market and workforce flexibility (Wickham, 1986). As Arnot
(1987) points out in a critical review of government policy, its stated
commitment to increased social equality was minimal and, according to David (1983), it could even be regarded as anti-feminist.

This MSC initiative came nearly 10 years after the passage of the

Sex Discrimination Act (1975) signalled the newest feminist campaign for sex equality in education. [Earlier campaigns had included the struggle for female access to secondary and higher education in the second half of the nineteenth century, and the fight by teachers for equal pay and against the marriage bar in the 1920s and 1930s (Purvis, 1981; Oram, 1987)]. Feminist teachers, in particular, used the letter and the spirit of the new legislation to push for changes in school policy and classroom practice at both local and national levels (Whyte *et al.*, 1985; Weiner and Arnot, 1987). When equal opportunities was adopted as one of the TVEI funding criteria, it was given a cautious welcome by feminist teachers (see, e.g. Millman, 1985). However, they were primarily concerned with increasing social equality. In contrast, the MSC's training target was the differentiated (by sex, class, etc.) labour market. How can this shared concern about equal opportunities by two apparent contrary forces be explained?

To explore this I shall first consider the variety of feminist teacher-led initiatives directed towards schooling since 1975. I shall then examine the ways in which equal opportunities has been adopted and defined within new government initiatives such as TVEI, etc. I shall focus, in particular, on the intentions of the policy makers. Overall, I shall question whether the ideological differences implicit in such concepts as 'equality' and 'vocationalism' are reconcilable, and what implications these tensions might have for feminist practitioners.

While I concentrate on the achievements of teachers, they did not work in isolation. They drew support from national research projects such as Girls into Science and Technology (1981–4), and the Schools Council Sex Differentiation Project (1981–3), and more recently from the Genderwatch materials developed in Merton. A number of local authorities were also particularly active in promoting gender equality (see Whyte *et al.*, 1985, for examples of this work).

The analysis I offer is critical in so far as it seeks to increase understanding about the origins and reasons for recent central government policies and the place of equal opportunities within them. In particular, I hope that it will enable those working on equality issues within the new initiatives to develop a firmer grasp of the 'politics' of their situation and, as a consequence, make more progress in their work.

Gaby Weiner

Developing educational policy on gender

My goal in this section is two-fold; first, to provide an indication of the immense diversity of projects and initiatives on gender and education since 1975 and, secondly, to show how ideas and strategies have developed. In order to make the task more manageable, I shall focus in particular on the ideas and strategies of those teachers who were 'pioneers' in the field, and who were active at the end of the 1970s through to the mid-1980s.

A historical overview of their achievements can best be represented as a sequence of activities and strategies. These include (a) establishing that gender inequalities exist; (b) initiating changes in school policy and classroom practice; (c) reflecting practically and theoretically on the different kinds of approaches available; and (d) implementing more developed equality strategies in schools.

Establishing the existence of gender inequalities

In the first instance, feminist teachers were concerned to raise awareness among their colleagues about the extent of gender inequalities in education. They focused on three areas in particular. They considered:

1 *Attitudes*: both of pupils and teachers, e.g. it was argued that while teachers believed that they treated boys and girls without prejudice, detailed investigation showed that this was not the case and that girls appeared to be seriously disadvantaged in the schooling system (Clarricoates, 1978; Spender, 1980; Stanworth, 1981; Kelly, 1981).
2 *School organization and resources*: for example, inequitable staffing patterns, sex-stereotyping in texts and reading schemes, and sex-specific patterns of subject choice at 13 plus (see, e.g. Whyld, 1983; Millman and Weiner, 1985).
3 *Activity of women in the labour force*: particularly on the statistical unlikelihood of women remaining in the home for most of their adult lives and the consequent need to change 'traditional' career choices of pupils (Joshi *et al.*, 1982; Avent, 1982).

Their findings were publicised in a variety of ways – in the form of written or verbal reports to school staff meetings, to school inservice conferences, or to evening seminars arranged by local 'women in education' groups. Feminist teachers also used their findings to lobby advisers and administrators for changes in policy and for practical support, e.g. in providing funding for the production of non-sexist teaching materials or the design of new courses. (Myers, 1982; Cornbleet and Libovitch, 1983).

Initiating changes

Once the 'problem' of gender inequality had been established, solutions were sought that could be readily injected into school life. *Ad hoc* strategies were developed which included:

- the creation of equal opportunities working parties and posts to devise 'whole-school' policies;
- revision of school materials (e.g. texts, reading schemes, examination questions and displays);
- raising 'awareness' about equality issues at staff, parents' and governors meetings;
- rearranging timetabling to enable pupils to opt more easily for non-traditional subjects such as physics for girls and modern languages for boys;
- appointing female senior staff to provide fresh role models for female pupils;
- encouraging wider career aspiration by inviting people holding non-traditional jobs into school; and
- changing school organization by, for instance, 'de-sexing' registers and 'uni-sexing' school uniform.

The main focus of teachers was upon school-based practical change; how could they help reduce inequalities between the sexes by changing their own and their colleagues' perceptions and practice? Yet the solutions were highly diverse. They stemmed not merely from local or individual priorities but also from critical differences in the perspectives of the teachers themselves.

Reflecting on differences in approach

By the early 1980s two different feminist teacher perspectives became discernible in the challenge to previous educational practices of gender differentiation: the 'equal opportunities' and 'anti-sexist' or 'girl-centred' approaches (Weiner, 1985).

Briefly, the equal opportunities approach aimed at reforms on behalf of girls and women, and sometimes boys and men, within the existing educational structure. The anti-sexist approach aimed at changing unequal power relations between the sexes by transforming the patriarchal and ethnocentric nature of school structures and curricula. These differences became evident in the strategies chosen by teachers to challenge sexist schooling.

The equal opportunities approach emphasized, for instance, persuading girls to go into scientific and technological occupations, textbook reform, a common curriculum and changing sex-stereotyped option choices. It emphasized equal female representation in the higher echelons of school and society. The anti-sexist approach, on the other hand, focused on combining anti-sexist and anti-racist strategies, challenging male school knowledge by considering what *her*story or girl-centred science might look like, and addressing the more contentious issues of sexuality, sexual harassment, heterosexuality and homophobia. Their concern was that of empowering female pupils and teachers in their struggle against the male domination of schooling.

While both approaches were feminist in that they wanted to improve educational opportunities for girls and women, they had different priorities for change. Those favouring equal opportunities opted for awareness raising and consensual change. They asked for increased inservice training as a means of ensuring recognition of sex equality as a professional issue. Anti-sexist teachers, in contrast, focused more on structural changes in their emphasis on the importance of unequal power relations and the need to address conflicting interests. They sought to challenge male domination of schooling by, for instance, establishing school girls' and women's support groups, designing 'girl-centred' curricula and replacing hierarchy, competitiveness and selection with cooperation and democracy. However, there were also disagreements of emphasis and strategy within anti-sexist approaches, i.e. between socialist, radical, black and lesbian feminists (see Weiner and Arnot, 1987, for a fuller discussion of this).

This dual classification has proved helpful in understanding why certain strategies were more attractive to some than others. However, critics (e.g. Acker, 1986) point to the difficulty, in practice, of identifying such clear differences in perspective and strategy. Despite theoretical differences teachers' initiatives crossed the boundaries between the two approaches, and teachers holding different perspectives formed alliances to strengthen their campaigns on behalf of girls and women.

It has become apparent in the last few years that experience of trying to implement change in schooling has brought the two approaches closer together. They have gained from each other and new strategies have emerged which combine features of both.

An alliance in policy and practice?

Recent strategies, most noticeable in the London area, have modified the two approaches, not for radical change, but for feasible and practical reform. The necessity of majority staff support for the effective implementation of change has led to an emphasis on developing 'whole-school' policy on gender. The discovery that it needs more than merely 'tinkering' with timetabling to make girls opt for 'male' subjects has stimulated deeper thinking about the underlying reasons for gender differentiation. Moreover, acknowledgement of the potential influence of inservice and of the continued need to raise awareness has led to the creation of a variety of school and authority courses and publications. These have enabled gender issues to be explored in greater depth by teachers outside the 'pioneering' cohort.

First, connections have been made between gender, race and class:

> Relationships between race, sex and class are dynamic and complex and have implications for classroom practice. If race, gender and class issues are compartmentalised, the teaching approaches and strategies developed for combatting racism, sexism and class bias will be limited and less effective than they might be. (Minhas, 1986)

Activities of teachers in this area have included developing policies which address racism and sexism across the curriculum, exploring girls' experiences of racism in school as a basis for change, and designing activities specifically for girls from different ethnic groups. For instance:

> On Monday evenings, we hold our girls' group. We needed it as there were no places for Bengali teenage girls to meet, apart from the school. Shejuti (an Asian youth project) filled a much-felt void. As well as providing us with a Youth Club, it enables us to explore through our discussion groups, the value of our culture, customs and way of life, as well as the positive aspects of living in British society. (The Young Women of Shejuti, 1986, p. 75)

Teachers have also focused on aspects of sexuality in and around school. For instance, they have organized conferences on sexism and sexuality for older secondary pupils, run workshops on assertion and confidence training for girls, and considered and redefined school policy on sexual harassment:

> Sexual harassment is not confined to uninvited groping and grabbing but extends to a range of interactions where boys exert power over girls and consequently deny girls rightful access to educational resources (eg teacher time, classroom space, play areas), freedom of expression, and perhaps most damagingly, reinforce in girls the submissive and 'sex-object' roles into which they are socialised by the family, the media and so on. (Parke, 1986, p. 112)

Other areas on which teachers have placed particular emphasis include revising the content of certain curriculum areas, e.g. history, social studies, science and religious education, to make them more 'sexually inclusive' (Yates, 1985); making science, computing, technical subjects and mathematics more accessible to girls; exploring school policy on language, general organization, classroom management and library usage; and developing equal opportunities policies in boys' schools (ILEA, 1986a,b).

In surveying the achievements of feminist teachers, whatever their perspective, there have been noticeable gaps. For instance, only recently has any attention been given to how to plan effectively for change (Myers, 1987). There appears to have been a failure to differentiate between short-term and long-term goals, i.e. to distinguish between, for example, the time needed to eradicate sexist comments from texts and that needed to alter pupil or teacher consciousness. Moreover, there have been few attempts to evaluate the achievements of work on gender, perhaps because aims have been overly ambitious resulting, at times, in disappointingly slow progress. Another possible reason is that teacher activists have tended to be women located at the lower levels of school hierarchies who have put all their (limited) energy and influence into achieving recognition of gender equality as an educational aim. They are also likely to have been excluded from, and therefore lacked experience of, formal institutional mechanisms of 'managing change'.

To summarize this section of the chapter, I have outlined the development of feminist ideas on educational priorities and their realization. I have described the achievements of the 'pioneer' teachers, their political commitment and their differences of approach. Though the national scene remains patchy, feminist teachers have made substantial progress in legitimizing equal opportunities as a mainstream education issue, particularly where institutional support has been provided by local authorities, and latterly through government initiatives such as TVEI.

In recent years, however, the context has altered in that central government has taken a much more directive stance towards education, particularly in its relationship with local authorities and teachers. This has affected its power to implement policies not only on equal opportunities but also on, for instance, curriculum, assessment and examinations, and teachers' conditions of service. This brings me to the second section of this chapter. Here I examine the implications of the new government 'vocational' initiatives for equal opportunities.

Vocationalism and equal opportunities

In contrast to the feminist initiatives described above, the theoretical underpinnings of the new government projects (some of which are examined in this book) have an entirely different source. They were designed to challenge existing educational provision 'with its peculiar combination of tradition, inertia and local autonomy' (Young, 1987) from a market-led, rather than a social justice, perspective, though some conservative politicians might argue that the goals of the two are ultimately the same. The appeal to change of the new projects, as the first chapter of this book indicates, has been unashamedly of the 'carrot-dangling' kind.

'Categorical' funding works in the following way. A policy is developed; extra funds are made available; voluntary cooperation is invited in exchange for a share of the resources; and acceptance of the resources is equated with acceptance of the policy. The ability to deliver is also assumed (Harland, 1987). Providing financial inducement as a means of promoting change is, however, far from new. What is different in the 1980s is the tightness of the cords which bind the funder and the funded. According to Harland, TVEI, for instance, emerged as a sophisticated strategy for delivering policy both as a technical, bureaucratic structure and as an initiative calculated to secure the desired response from those who implement it.

Though pioneered by the MSC through TVEI in 1983 and in TRIST (TVEI Related Inservice Training) in 1986, this model of educational change was also adopted by the DES in the Lower-Attaining Pupils Programme (LAPP) in 1983, the Records of Achievement Project in 1984, and GRIST (Grant Related Inservice Training) in 1987. Few have been surprised at the degree of take-up of these projects in the mid-1980s when general finance levels were low.

In offering support for equal opportunities within these schemes, educational policy-makers, particularly within the MSC, demonstrated that equality issues were beginning to be perceived as pertinent to the government's wider vocational project. In the case where local authorities were already pursuing equal opportunities policies and were consequently anxious to incorporate them into the new initiatives, LEA priorities for change were likely to be determined to some extent by the vocational ethos of the schemes.

To understand the implications for equal opportunities of the new initiatives, it seems worth considering how this new 1980s brand of vocationalism differs from earlier concerns about vocational education. First, it has its origin specifically in the developing crisis of economic productivity of industry in the 1970s, and according to Young (1987) is an attempt to locate both the cause and the solution of that crisis in the failure of the education system to meet industrial needs. Accordingly, the new vocational policies were responses by government to the alleged failure of education and training. Various shifts were discernible, including:

- an increasingly directive role for central government, and a parallel attack on local autonomy;
- a change in focus of the educational debate to an emphasis on standards and quality (value for money!) and away from concerns about availability and distribution of opportunities; and
- increased disenchantment with the subject-based school curriculum as irrelevant to the needs of a substantial proportion of the school population.

It is clear that TVEI, TRIST, LAPP and Records of Achievement all contain some elements of vocationalism, as depicted above. When set up emphasis was placed on quality and standards rather than equality of access and outcome; they are directly funded by central government; and they attempt to move away from conventional knowledges and skills.

That previous forms of schooling failed large numbers of children cannot be denied, this providing the basis for the feminist challenge to education. Some have suggested that the fast changing educational landscape might possibly enhance opportunities:

> They [government policy makers] suggest at least an attempt to shift from a top-down bureaucratic system with limited access to any who is not an academic success in school. The question is whether these moves to a more open market centred system of education will lead to new opportunities or . . . (to) new forms of closure. (Young, 1987, p. 80)

But others are more pessimistic about whether the new educational policies will improve matters. For instance, it has been claimed that the new policies will prove yet more divisive:

> This 'new vocationalism' signals the abandonment of equal opportunity as a central reference point of educational strategy. The key element of these schemes is out-of-school work experience, and their guiding philosophy is to create an appropriate education for certain types of students, to be derived largely from their assumed destination in the division of labour. (Finn, 1985, p. 113)

Given that there has been a move away from concerns about the redistribution of opportunities in the 1980s in most areas of government policy, and given that there has been no prioritization of 'women's issues', I find it puzzling that equality of opportunity in education has merited such attention, particularly from the MSC.

Given the vocational orientation of TVEI, etc., the benefit of the economy must be the principal reason. As I have already suggested, vocational policies have aimed at making education more responsive to the 'needs' of the capitalist economy. It could be argued that equal opportunities criteria were injected into TVEI because of the perceived need for a free (that is, unsegmented) labour market to serve the interests of the economy. Schooling's 'delivery' of a flexible workforce – undifferentiated by sex (etc.) – would make adaptation to future changes in the manufacturing and service industries much more practicable. Although no such criteria exist within LAPP or Records of Achievement, in so far as these initiatives can be said to espouse vocationalism, they provide a context in which the same arguments can be raised.

Historical comparisons are useful here. Hamilton reports that in the late nineteenth century discussion about vocational education centred almost entirely around two callings:

marriage and motherhood on the one hand and the 'liberal' profes-
sions on the other. . . . The confinement of motherhood, like a
posting in the far-flung colonies, was recognised as a call to 'higher
things' – the disinterested service of the British Empire. (Hamilton,
1987, p. 4)

A more recent parallel might be that the new vocational emphasis
on broad-based skills and knowledges rather than 'traditional'
academic subjects effectively means that teachers and female pupils
are being 're-packaged' for the benefit (or in the 'disinterested
service') of the labour market. The current *educational* focus on
removing sex-stereotyping say, from texts and option choices,
shows a marked contrast to perceptions of a century earlier. Then,
'feminine' qualities, appropriate for wifedom and motherhood, were
harnessed to the needs of the Empire; now they are being questioned
in relation to the economy of the 1980s, certainly in the context of
education.

Moreover, if the object of vocationalism is to regenerate the
economy through education, the fewer the barriers to creating
skilled labour the better. The removal of previous social barriers to
educational advancement through promotion of equal opportunities
is likely to yield economic benefits to both the individual and the
state. Thus an 'equal opportunities' emphasis, whether based on
gender, race or class, which increases the pool of available technologists, science teachers or market executives, seems eminently
sensible.

As has already been mentioned, in order to achieve the desired
shift towards vocationalism, government has sought to extend its
control of the education system. Lawton and Chitty claim that,
additionally, the government has chosen 'bureaucratic' rather than
'professional' modes of working within education:

> The bureaucratic approach . . . is concerned with the 'efficiency' of
> the whole system. . . . It is concerned with controlling what is taught
> in schools and making teachers generally more accountable to central
> authority . . . (it) concentrates on output and testing. . . . The profes-
> sional curriculum represents concern with the quality of the teaching
> process and with the needs of individual children. (Lawton and
> Chitty, 1987, p. 5)

The bureaucratic (or vocational) approach reflects the 'free-
market' philosophies of the New Right; it evaluates schooling in rela-

tion to its contribution to national prosperity. The professional approach, on the other hand, focuses on the 'quality of input and the skills, knowledge and awareness of the teacher . . . on individual differences and the learning process'; it identifies education as an individual right and of intrinsic value. Many would argue, as do Lawton and Chitty, for the professional approach as more appropriate for schooling, both ethically and educationally. Choices are less clear for feminists, however, since the assumptions and behaviour underpinning past professional practices in education have drawn strong feminist criticism (e.g. Davidson, 1985; Marshall, 1985). It could be argued that bureaucratic/vocational policies are more 'girl-friendly' since equal opportunities have been more highly prioritized by them. In contrast, 'professional' approaches have proved highly resistant, although more recently they have accepted feminist analyses as part of the wider educational debate.

It is not only the policies but the practical applications that separate the new vocationalism from its predecessors. What does vocationalism mean, in practice and for the role of teachers? This has been explored in some depth by researchers and evaluators involved in TVEI..

> Our use of the term 'vocationalism' . . . includes all aspects of institutionalised educational practices that consciously and explicitly relate learning experiences to post-school 'adult' occupations that do not necessarily involve paid employment . . . we see 'vocationalism' predominantly as an approach or orientation within schools, rather than as identifiable sets of innovative procedures that are somehow auxiliary to established forms of provision. (Sikes and Taylor, 1987, p. 57)

The vocational 'orientation' to which Sikes and Taylor refer is significant in its apparent rejection of 'chalk and talk' in favour of group tasks and assignments. It also emphasizes individual development and peer and institutional socialization above knowledge acquisition. There is also, according to Young (1987), a marked preference for modular frameworks specifying learning outcomes and mastery of skills related to specific occupational groupings (e.g. production, services, retail) over subject-based syllabi. The intention, it seems, is both to extend access to those who have been disaffected by conventional schooling and to 'socialize' the prospective workforce into accepting responsibility for its uncertain future.

It is clear, then, that within TVEI and TRIST, emphasis on the role of education in 'delivering' the skills and knowledges necessary for the regeneration of economic prosperity typifies current changes in educational thinking. The frequent use of such terms as 'delivery' and 'package' illustrates a new language associated with the vocational ethos. Few teachers would have considered using such terminology prior to the onset of vocationalism, yet it is now used routinely by teachers and administrators. It marks a break with the 'professional' language of educators and implies that teachers are now only part of the schooling production process. Teachers are now perceived as intermediaries (or operatives) between the curriculum/policy-makers and the pupil/consumers. Harland (1986) draws a parallel between the current role of teachers, and encyclopaedia salesmen (salespeople?) whose freedom and autonomy consists in exercising their powers of persuasion to sell a product in whose content they have had only a superficial input.

This has contradictory implications for feminist teachers. On the one hand, if equal opportunities policies achieve a secure place within the new schemes, there is more likelihood of successful implementation – teachers will be obliged to address the issues, if only superficially. On the other hand, failure to 'deliver' changes in, say, option choices or stereotyped career patterns, in the limited period offered by the schemes, might put government support for equal opportunities in jeopardy. The experience of the earlier feminist initiatives is that change, particularly in awareness and acceptance of sex equality as an educational priority, can be painfully slow. This form of change process seems incompatible with the deliberately fast pace and short-term nature of the government schemes.

While the new 'vocational' language is not evident in all government schemes, the central issue of the redefinition of the teacher's role remains important. In LAPP and Records of Achievement, for instance, teachers' autonomy is affected by both the short-term nature of the schemes and the overall control by government. Both schemes also utilize a 'progressive' educational language of 'student-centred learning' and 'negotiated' curricula. It could be argued that this progressive language is part of the vocational pedagogy mentioned earlier that seeks to extend access and to 'socialize' hitherto alienated or excluded students.

Feminism and vocationalism

In this chapter I have concentrated on the practice of feminist teachers and on the intentions of vocational policy-makers. I have attempted to show the implications (and the contradictions) of support for equal opportunities within the new government initiatives. Given its overriding concern with schooling's relationship to the labour market, e.g. the need for more technologists and science specialists, the vocational perspective on equal opportunities is likely to value 'equal opportunities' above 'anti-sexist' strategies. This has dictated the modes of operation available to those working on equal opportunities within the new schemes, as the case studies in this volume indicate. At a practical level, then, 'liberal'/progressive ideas concerning freedom for girls and women to move upwards in educational and occupational hierarchies have become synonymous with 'liberal' *laissez-faire* ideas about labour market freedom.

In locating equal opportunities within the new initiatives, I suggest that we are entering a new era of gender politics in education. The more 'radical' edge of feminist activity seems to have little future but there is now a stronger institutional base than ever before for equal opportunities work.

In deciding whether, and on what conditions, to become involved with equal opportunities developments within the new vocationalism, feminists might consider the following questions. Is there any difference between the 'liberal' approach to equal opportunities of vocational policy-makers and that of feminist teachers advocating 'girl-friendly' schooling? (See Whyte *et al.*, 1985). Can feminists draw on earlier gender initiatives to give equality a higher priority in the new government schemes and to implement more effective strategies for change? Can feminists create a new power base in the new education programmes?

It seems that feminists have been provided with a foothold in the new system, which they never had in the old. The problem now is, how can it best be exploited.

Postscript

During the period in which this book has been written we have seen the development of proposals for further massive changes in our education system. In 1988, the new Education Act signalled the greatest revolution in this system since the Education Act of 1944. The legislation detailed far-reaching changes in:

1 The school curriculum, via a framework of core and foundation subjects, each with its associated nationally prescribed attainment targets and assessments at 7, 11, 14 and 16.
2 The degree of autonomy of individual schools through arrangements for the setting up of grant-maintained schools (allowing for schools to 'opt out' of LEA control), local management of schools and changed arrangements for admission of pupils to maintained schools.

As we write this postscript, the implications of these proposals for technical and vocational education, for the development of records of achievement and for curricular developments for lower-attaining pupils have yet to be worked out. A tension is already apparent between the national curriculum proposals with their strong emphasis upon traditional subject areas and the cross-curricular dimension evident in many developments resulting from the new national initiatives. Nevertheless, there is no doubt that the TVEI and Records of Achievement initiatives will continue. The consultation document on the national curriculum (DES, 1987a) states how the national extension of TVEI will also help LEAs in the development and establishment of the national curriculum, particularly in the areas of science and technology, and in enhancing the curriculum's relevance to adult and working life (p. 31). In the case of

Records of Achievement too, the DES, in their interim report on the pilot projects (DES, 1987b), indicates the link with the national curriculum, seeing both as 'concerned with identifying goals, designing a curriculum to meet those goals and recording pupils' positive achievements in relation to them' (p. 5). It is clear, therefore, that the gender implications of these initiatives remain important areas for analysis and debate.

Additionally, it must be recognized that there may be some gains for promotion of gender equality in the existence of a national curriculum. Here is not the place to examine this issue in detail, suffice it to say that if the proposals for core and foundation subjects are backed by a commitment on the part of the DES to equal access to the *same curriculum*, as advocated by the EOC in its response to the consultation document (EOC, 1987), then it could have positive outcomes for gender equality in schools. To support this, teachers responsible for 'delivering' the national curriculum would need to take part in inservice training programmes aimed at raising their awareness of gender issues in both the 'formal' and 'hidden' curriculum. This level of commitment would clearly have financial implications as all schools would need to make provision for teaching core and foundation subjects to all pupils; this would be likely to have a particularly significant effect upon single-sex schools which would need to make their own provisions for teaching all subjects.

Although there will clearly be some continuity between the curriculum developments associated with the national initiatives focused upon within this book and the national curriculum framework, there is a sharp contrast between the strategies for change revealed in these pilot projects and those consonant with greater central control through legislative powers. The model of change common to the four national initiatives was one premissed upon flexibility in response to local definitions of the issues. As Makins (1988) points out in reflecting upon the implications of the national curriculum for a local LAPP project, 'unless the new curriculum regulations allow for the kind of flexibility and experiment that is going on. . . , a great many students are likely to gain very little from their last two years of compulsory schooling' (p. 23). Such flexibility has given LEAs quite a significant role in the process of change within these initiatives, one which, as the case studies in this book reveal, has been important in the promotion of greater gender equality. With greater autonomy for individual schools, and a consequent waning of the powers of LEAs, it is likely that the potential influence of LEA equal opportunities policies will become more limited in scope. Moreover, any diminution in the role played by some LEAs in supporting the development of a 'bank of expertise' on gender issues would be a sad loss; the disbandment of the ILEA is a particular case in point.

To maximize the opportunities for promotion of greater equality in the new context of the Education Act will require a careful analysis of appropriate strategies for bringing about change. Greater school autonomy suggests that the views of headteachers, governors and parents will become more significant. The degree of awareness of gender issues on the part of these groups will be critical and the case studies indicate that one way of achieving this is through the presentation of data on differences in pupil performance. Collection and publication of data, not only on sex differentiation in pupil performance but also in relation to areas of spending in schools, will be a central responsibility for all schools in the future. The EOC has recommended that:

> information is required to be provided in such a way that it is possible for parents and other interested parties to identify the amount spent on girls and boys respectively, particularly where single sex options (e.g. in TVEI) and single sex activities (e.g. girls' choir and boys' football) are maintained. (EOC, 1987, p. 2).

The possibility of an increasing isolation of schools from each other and the consequent diminution of local networks of support may also affect strategies for promotion of gender equality; it is notable that teachers in the project case studies became most effective when developing materials and strategies alongside others. In a situation of greater central control of the education system, there will be a need to find other sources of legitimation and support for work on gender issues. In response to the various DES consultation documents relating to the proposed legislation, the EOC makes a number of recommendations suggesting a greater responsibility for the Department in securing equality of opportunity; for example, that:

> the monitoring, inspection and enforcement of the national curriculum should include formal assessment of the extent to which equality of opportunity for girls and boys is being secured. (EOC, 1987a, p. 10)

This shift towards a 'coherent national policy for equality of opportunity' as referred to by Carr (1985), though welcome, would need to be complemented by real opportunities for practitioners to formulate their own definitions of the issues and strategies for change. As Harland (1987) has argued, in discussing the responses of practitioners to increased central control via TVEI, it is important to maximize the 'vitality of the practitioner' within a coherent national policy through ensuring a powerful professional input at the centre. Any such input fuelling central government thinking on gender issues in the national curriculum must rest ultimately upon the opportunity for sound analysis and development work at grassroots level; such has been the challenge and the opportunity taken up by the pilot projects presented in this book.

Bibliography

Acker, S. (1986). 'What feminists want from education', in Hartnett, A. and Naish, M. (eds), *Education and Society Today*. Falmer, Brighton.

Arnot, M. (1987). 'Political lip-service or radical reform? Central government responses to sex equality as a policy issue', in Arnot, M. and Weiner, G. (eds), *Gender and the Politics of Schooling*. Hutchinson, London.

Avent, C. (1982). 'Careers education and guidance'. *Secondary Education Journal*, **12** (2), 6–7.

Barlow, N. (1986). 'TRIST and the Future of In-service Training'. *Forum* **29** (1). 6–8.

Batts, D., Davis, B. and Jenkins, D. (1985). *Initiative: Take One*. University of Warwick.

Batts, D., Davis, B. and Jenkins, D. (1986). *Initiative : Take Two*, University of Warwick.

Cant, A. (1985). 'Development of LEA Policy: Manchester', in Whyte, J., Deem, R., Kant, L. and Cruickshank, M. (eds), *Girl-Friendly Schooling*. Methuen, London.

Carr, L. (1985). 'Legislation and mediation: to what extent has the Sex Discrimination Act changed girls' schooling?' in Whyte, J., Deem, R., Kant, L. and Cruickshank, M. (eds), *Girl-Friendly Schooling*. Methuen, London.

Carr, L. (1987). 'Equal opportunities and TVEI', in *TVEI Developments 2: Equal Opportunities*. MSC, London.

Clarricoates, K. (1978). 'Dinosaurs in the classroom: a re-examination of some aspects of the hidden curriculum in primary schools'. *Women's Studies International Quarterly*, **1**, 4.

Cornbleet, A. and Libovitch, S. (1983). 'Anti-sexist initiatives in a mixed comprehensive school: a case study', in Wolpe, A. M. and Donald, J. (eds), *Is There Anyone Here from Education?* Pluto Press, London.

Coventry City Council (1982). *Comprehensive Education for Life*. Coventry City Council, Coventry.

Coventry City Council (1983). *Towards Equal Opportunities in Secondary School: What Does it Mean for Girls?* Education Department, Coventry City Council, Coventry.

Coventry City Council (1984a). *Future Choices: Problems and Opportunities.* Coventry City Council, Coventry.

Coventry City Council (1984b). *DES Special Project: A Report on Equal Opportunities.* Education Department, Coventry City Council, Coventry.

Coventry City Council (1985). *Future Choices: Meeting the Challenges.* Coventry City Council, Coventry.

Coventry City Council (1986). *TVEI Annual Report.* Education Department, Coventry City Council, Coventry.

Coventry City Council (1987). *Economic Monitor.* Coventry City Council, Coventry.

Dale, R. (1985). 'The background and inception of the Technical and Vocational Education Initiative', in Dale, R. (ed.), *Education, Training and Employment; Towards a New Vocationalism?* Pergamon, Oxford.

David, M. (1983). 'Thatcherism *is* anti-feminism'. *Trouble and Strife.* 1 (Winter), 44–8.

Davidson, H. (1985). 'Unfriendly myths about women teachers', in Whyte, J., Deem, R., Kant, L. and Cruickshank, M. (eds), *Girl-Friendly Schooling.* Methuen, London.

Davin, A. (1979). 'Mind that you do as you are told: reading books for board school girls'. *Feminist Review,* 3.

Deem, R. (1987). 'Bringing gender equality into schools', in Walker, S. and Barton, L. (eds), *Changing Policies, Changing Teachers: New Directions for Schooling?* Open University Press, Milton Keynes.

Department of Education and Science (1986). *Report by HM Inspectors on a Survey of the Lower Attaining Pupils Programme: The First Two Years.* Department of Education and Science, London.

Department of Education and Science/Department of Employment (1986). *Working Together – Education and Training.* Joint White Paper. Cmnd 9823. HMSO, London.

Department of Education and Science/Welsh Office (1987a). *The National Curriculum 5 – 16: A Consultation Document.* Department of Education and Science, London.

Department of Education and Science/Welsh Office (1987b). *Records of Achievement: An Interim Report.* HMSO, London.

Equal Opportunities Commission (1983). *Formal Investigation Report: Sidney Stringer School and Community College, Coventry.* Equal Opportunities Commission, London.

Equal Opportunities Commission (1987a). *Response of the Equal Opportunities Commission to the Consultation Document: The National Curriculum 5–16.* Equal Opportunities Commission, London.

Equal Opportunities Commission (1987b). *Response by the Equal*

Opportunities Commission to the Consultative Paper: Financial Delegation to Schools. Equal Opportunities Commission, London.

Finn, D. (1985). 'The Manpower Services Commission and the Youth Training Scheme: a permanent bridge to work', in Dale R. (ed.), *Education, Training and Employment.* Pergamon, Oxford.

Hamilton, D. (1987). *What is a Vocational Curriculum?* Paper presented to the annual conference of the British Educational Research Association, Manchester.

Harland, J. (1986). 'The new inset: a transformation scene'. *Journal of Educational Policy*, **2**, (3), 235–44.

Harland, J. (1987). 'The TVEI experience: issues of control, response and the professional role of teachers', in Gleeson, D. (ed.), *TVEI and Secondary Education: A Critical Appraisal.* Open University Press, Milton Keynes.

Haywood, R. and Wootten, M. (1987). 'The Gateshead LAPP: prevocational education in a cold climate'. *Forum*, **29** (3), 82–4.

Headlam-Wells, J. (1985). 'Humberside goes neuter: an example of LEA intervention for equal opportunities', in Whyte, J., Deem, R., Kant, L. and Cruickshank, M. (eds) *Girl-Friendly Schooling.* Methuen, London.

Hopkins, D. (1986). 'Recent developments in secondary education: some premature reflections'. *Cambridge Journal of Education*, **16** (3), 195–210.

Inner London Education Authority (1986a). *Primary Matters.* ILEA, London.

Inner London Education Authority (1986b). *Secondary Issues.* ILEA, London.

Joshi, H., Layard, R. and Owen, S. (1982). *Female Labour Supply in Postwar Britain.* Centre for Labour Economics, London School of Economics, London.

Kelly, A. (ed.) (1981). *The Missing Half; Girls and Science Education.* Manchester University Press, Manchester.

Kelly, A., Whyte, J. and Smail, B. (1984). *Girls into Science and Technology: Final Report.* University of Manchester, Manchester.

Langley, K. M. (1986). *Gender Issues in the 14–16 Curriculum Project in Northamptonshire.* Paper presented at the annual conference of the British Educational Research Association, Bristol.

Lawton, D. and Chitty, C. (1987). 'Towards a national curriculum'. *Forum*, **30** (1), 4–5.

Luxton, R. (1986). *Participation of Girls in TVEI.* Hertfordshire County Council.

Makins, V. (1988). Tailor-made transitions. *Times Educational Supplement*, 26 February.

Manpower Services Commission (1984a). *TVEI; Annual Review.* MSC, London.

Manpower Services Commission (1984b). *Regional Workshop Papers.* MSC, Sheffield.

Manpower Services Commission (1985). *Regional Workshop Papers.* MSC, Sheffield.

Manpower Services Commission (1987). *TVEI Developments 2: Equal Opportunities*. MSC, London.

Manpower Services Commission (1988). *Directory of TRIST Practice*. MSC, London.

Marshall, C. (1985). 'The stigmatised woman: the professional woman in a male sex-typed career'. *Journal of Educational Administration*, **23** (2), 131–52.

McCulloch, G. (1987). 'History and policy: the politics of TVEI', in Gleeson, D. (ed.), *TVEI and Secondary Education; A Critical Appraisal*. Open University Press, Milton Keynes.

McIntyre, T. (1987). *Equal Opportunities for Boys and Girls in TVEI. An Evaluation Progress Report*. MSC, TVEI Unit, London.

Merson, M. (1987). *Coventry TVEI Report*. University of Warwick.

Millman, V. (1985). 'The new vocationalism in secondary schools: its influence on girls', in Whyte, J., Deem, R., Kant, L. and Cruickshank, M. (eds), *Girl-Friendly Schooling*. Methuen, London.

Millman, V. (1987). *Equal Opportunities: The Role of the Professional Tutor in the Promotion of Sex Equality*. Education Department, Coventry City Council, Coventry.

Millman, V. and Weiner, G. (1985). *Sex Differentiation in Schooling; is there really a problem?* Longmans Schools Council, London.

Millman, V. and Weiner, G. (1987). 'Engendering equal opportunities: the case of TVEI', in Gleeson, D. (ed.), *TVEI and Secondary Education, A Critical Appraisal*. Open University Press, Milton Keynes.

Minhas, R. (1986). 'Race, gender and class – making the connections', in ILEA (ed.), *Secondary Issues*. ILEA, London.

Myers, K. (1982). 'Equal opportunities in Haverstock School', in EOC (ed.), *Gender and the Secondary Curriculum. EOC Research Bulletin 6*, Spring. EOC, Manchester.

Myers, K. (ed.) (1987). *Genderwatch*. EOC/SCDC, Manchester.

North-West TRIST (1987). *Gender Equality: a Professional Issue*, Tameside and Rochdale Equal Opportunities, MSC, London.

NUT (Coventry Branch) (1984). *Primary Teachers in Coventry*. Coventry NUT, Coventry.

OCEA (1985). *Provisional OCEA Handbook*. University of Oxford Delegacy of Local Examination, Oxford.

O'Neill, S. (1987). 'Records of achievement: pupil profiles', in Myers, K. (ed.), *Genderwatch*. EOC/SCDC, Manchester.

Oram, A. (1987). 'Sex antagonism in the teaching profession: equal pay and the marriage bar 1910–39', in Arnot, M. and Weiner, G. (eds), *Gender and the Politics of Schooling*. Hutchinson, London.

Orr, P. (1985). 'Sex bias in schools: national perspectives', in Whyte, J., Deem, R., Kant, L. and Cruickshank, M. (eds), *Girl-Friendly Schooling*. Methuen, London.

Parke, S. (1986). 'Girls and sexual harassment – an issue for school policy', in ILEA (ed.) *Secondary Issues*. ILEA, London.

PRAISE (Pilot Records of Achievement in Schools Evaluation) (1987). *Interim Evaluation Report.* Open University/University of Bristol, Milton Keynes/Bristol.

Purvis, J. (1981). 'Towards a history of women's education in nineteenth century Britain: a sociological analysis'. *Westminster Studies,* 4, 45–71.

Sikes, P. and Taylor, M. (1987). 'Some problems with defining, interpreting and communicating vocational education', in Gleeson D. (ed.), *TVEI and Secondary Education: A Critical Appraisal.* Open University Press, Milton Keynes.

Spender, D. (1980). *Man Made Language.* RKP, London.

Stanworth, M. (1981). *Gender and Schooling: A Study of Sexual Division in the Classroom.* Hutchinson, London.

Taylor, H. (1985). 'INSET for equal opportunities in the London Borough of Brent', in Whyte J., Deem, R., Kant, L. and Cruickshank, M. (eds), *Girl-Friendly Schooling.* Methuen, London.

Taylor, H. (1987). 'The redefinition of equality of opportunity'. *Educational Management and Administration,* 16, 13–18.

Times Educational Supplement (1982). Report on the Ninth Annual Conference of the Council of Local Education Authorities, Sheffield, 23 July, p. 12.

Weiner, G. (1985). 'Equal opportunities, feminism and girls' education: introduction', in Weiner, G. (ed.), *Just a Bunch of Girls: Feminist Approaches to Schooling.* Open University Press, Milton Keynes.

Weiner, G. and Arnot, M. (1987). 'Teachers and gender politics', in Arnot M. and Weiner, G. (eds), *Gender and the Politics of Schooling.* Hutchinson, London.

Weston, P. (1986). 'If success had many faces'. *Forum,* 28 (3), 79–81.

Whyld J. (ed.) (1983). *Sexism and the Secondary Curriculum.* Harper and Row, London.

Whyte, J.(1985). 'Girl-friendly science and the girl-friendly school', in Whyte, J., Deem, R., Kant, L. and Cruickshank, M., (1985). *Girl-Friendly Schooling.* Methuen, London.

Whyte, J., Deem, R., Kant, L. and Cruickshank, M. (eds) (1985). *Girl-Friendly Schooling.* Methuen, London.

Wickham, A. (1986). *Women and Training.* Open University Press, Milton Keynes.

Williams, R. (1961). *The Long Revolution.* Chatto and Windus, London.

Yates, L. (1985). 'Is girl-friendly schooling really what girls need?', in Whyte, J., Deem, R., Kant, L. and Cruickshank, M. (eds), *Girl-Friendly Schooling.* Methuen, London.

Young, M. (1987). 'Vocationalising tendencies in recent UK educational policy – sources of closure or sources of empowerment'. *Bildung und Erziehung,* March.

Young Women of Shejuti (1986). 'Shejuti', in ILEA (eds), *Secondary Issues.* ILEA, London.

Index